Twelve Stones

REMEMBERING THE GOD MOMENTS

LAURA PAYNE

ISBN: 1492352349
ISBN-13: 978-1492352341

FOR NIKA AND KEVIN

This is written for you two, my pride and joy. What I want more that anything else is for you both to walk closely with the Lord and to remember all that God has done for us. May you pass these God moments, as well as your own, on to your future kids and grandkids to encourage the next generation to praise and follow the Lord.

A Word of Thanks

I'd like to thank my husband, Steve, for the many hours he has poured into this book to make it read better and to get it ready for publishing. I never intended this book to go beyond the coffee table in our living room, but he saw that it could be an encouragement to others. So thank you, my lover and my friend, for getting me out of my comfort zone for the glory of God.

Table of Contents

Foreword

I was walking on Gold Beach a few years back when I noticed some flat, round stones along the shoreline. I gathered a bucketful with the hope of writing on each one a memory of a special thing that God has done in my life. God moments.

God likes us to remember what He has done. He told Moses to write on a scroll the amazing victory He had given against the Amalekites so that Joshua, Israel's future leader, would remember and trust God in upcoming battles. And then Joshua passed down to the next generation what God had done in his life by taking 12 stones from the middle of the Jordan River and setting them up as a remembrance of how God made a way for the whole Israelite community to cross the flooding river on dry ground. Passing on what God has done from one generation to the next gives courage to those who follow. It encourages them to trust, love and commit their lives to the One who does awesome deeds for those who love Him.

So over the next few years, I read through my journals, picking out the times when God had done something special on my behalf. I wrote on the stones the date and a summary of those "God moments". The stones rested on a ceramic plate on a table in our living room. If anyone asked me, I could give the full story behind each stone.

Then I was diagnosed with stage 4 melanoma and I thought to myself, "If God chooses to take me home, I won't be around to tell people the God stories behind each of the stones." That gave me the idea to write out the stories and put them next to my plate of stones, so that anyone who came over could pick up a stone and then look up the corresponding story in the book. Thankfully God has healed me of cancer, but since life is short anyway, I felt an urgency to finish this project. In that way, no matter when my last day on earth comes, there will be a history of God's faithfulness to me left behind to encourage my kids and the next generation.

There would be no book without God. He has done some amazing things in my life, and I can only stand back and say, "God, You are so awesome!" As it says in Psalm 106:2,

"Who can proclaim the mighty acts of the Lord
or fully declare his praise?"

May this book of God moments from my first 50 years of life bring You all the praise, Lord Jesus! I love You with all my heart!

Laura Payne

A Changed Heart

1970; 1975

<u>STONE:</u>

Asked God to show Himself to be the God of miracles if He was alive today. Answered in Mrs. Wood's Sunday School class.

I was brought to Pilgrim Baptist Church every Sunday from the time I was born. I didn't really enjoy going every week but I went without complaining. When some of my Sunday School classmates were getting baptized at age 8, my parents asked if I also wanted to be baptized. I told them no. In my heart I was struggling. The story of the Bible seemed to make sense, but was God really alive today as He had been back in the days the Bible was written? So I told God, "If You show me that You are still the God of miracles today, I will believe in You."

Five years passed and it was the fall of my 13th year. We had just changed Sunday School teachers and now our teacher was the pastor's wife, Ruth Wood. All that fall she would first teach her Sunday School lesson, and then add a personal story of how God was working in her life. After weeks of her miraculous stories of God's intervention, I realized that God had changed my heart. I remember sitting there at the end of a class and during the prayer time just quietly thanking God that He really was real and that I was His.

From that day on, life was not the same. There was a joy and peace that entered my heart that I had never known before. Previously I could hardly stand going to church. Now I was dragging my parents to both Sunday and Wednesday evening services. Before, I never read the Bible at home. Now I was reading it every day and LOVING my time with the Lord. As a matter of fact, the Word of God became my best friend through high school. He truly is the God of miracles today!

A Broken Arm

March 8, 1976

About six months after becoming a Christian, I was working on becoming the woman athlete of the year at my junior high school. In order to receive the award, one has to be on the all-star teams of every after-school sport they have during the school year. I had already done that for all the previous sports, but now they had just chosen the all-stars for basketball, and I hadn't been selected.

I thought I was good enough to be on the basketball all-star team, but for some reason Mrs. Roberts, the PE teacher, didn't choose me. The week I found out I was devastated, and I started praying every night that God would somehow put me on that team. For three nights I asked God to do that for me, knowing in my heart that He could do it.

On the morning of the fourth day, I got on the bus and at the next stop Susan Russwig climbed on with her arm in a cast. She was one of those chosen for the all-star team. I immediately thought, "Could God be answering my prayers?" But I knew there were already more than enough players on the team, so they wouldn't need a replacement for her. But later that day at school, Mrs. Roberts asked me if I would replace Susan on the team.

This was God's first miracle in my life after I became a Christian. I did end up getting woman athlete of the year, and God had made it possible!

A Heavenly Visit

1979

STONE:

Seeing an angel of the Lord in my bedroom in the middle of the night. Lay prostrate.

I t was my junior year in high school and I had my prom dress hanging on the back of the door in my bedroom. In the middle of the night, I woke up to a brilliantly gleaming person/angel in the corner of my room by the door where my dress hung. I remember immediately getting out of bed and lying prostrate on the carpet before this gleaming being. I even remember how odd it was at the time that the door seemed so far away from where I was lying, because if I were really lying on the floor before this angelic being, I should have been almost touching the door. But somehow there was plenty of room between me and the brilliant one, as if I were in another dimension.

After what seemed like a minute of awe and reverence, I looked up from the ground and realized I was alone, back in my small room. I returned to bed thinking how amazing the whole experience had been, and how God was encouraging me on in my walk with Him.

Laying Down Dreams

1980-1982

STONE:

Gave tennis up to God by going to Gordon College. God gave it back to me by allowing me to play on the men's team.

I recall that during my senior year of high school, my friends and tennis coaches encouraged me to apply to colleges for a tennis scholarship. I thought how cool that would be to play on a college team – a dream come true, since tennis was something I loved so much. But the Lord started speaking to my heart about going to a Christian college, so I looked at three of them on the East Coast: King's College, Houghton College, and Gordon College.

After visiting each, it was obvious that I was to go to Gordon. I contacted the athletic department to see if I could possibly get a tennis scholarship to help pay for school. The tennis coach wasn't in that day but the field hockey coach was. She told me there were no scholarships for tennis but that there were some available for field hockey. She knew of my field hockey career in high school and said she could give me a scholarship if I would play on her field hockey team (which would mean giving up tennis, since both tennis and field hockey were fall sports).

I had never thought that I WOULDN'T play tennis in college, but it was clear to me that I was to go to Gordon, and it was also obvious that I needed the scholarship. So I ended up playing field hockey at Gordon and not women's tennis. From my perspective, I had given up my dream of playing tennis in college in order to obey the Lord.

In the spring semester of my freshman year, the women's tennis team organized some unofficial, off-season matches, and one of the team members asked me to join them. I played #1 singles for that short time. During that season, some of the guys on the men's tennis team saw how I played and invited me to join them at their indoor practices later that year. After a few

4

times playing with them, all the guys were trying to figure out a way to keep me on their team for their spring season. I then had the best of both worlds: having a field hockey scholarship to help pay for the school where I felt God had led me, AND playing with the best tennis players at the school by being on the men's tennis team!

God was so good! I gave up my love of tennis to follow Him, and He blessed me beyond what I could have imagined!

Changed Plans

October 14, 1981

<u>STONE:</u>

Had plans to do LaVida (Interface) the summer of 1982. God changed my heart to do a missions trip to the Dominican Republic (flyer in mailbox, then chapel).

It was the fall semester of my sophomore year and I was already planning for the following summer to do Gordon's 2-week wilderness adventure camp (LaVida/Interface). I had wanted to do the camp ever since I heard about it from my roommate, Lotty Wagner. But God had other plans.

I went to my mailbox one day in mid-October and found a flyer about a missions trip that Gordon was sponsoring to the Dominican Republic. Missions was something I had never been interested in doing. But God had other plans and right then started tugging at my heart that I was supposed to do the missions trip and not the adventure camp.

After picking up my mail, I headed over to chapel. And who should be speaking that day but the guy who was putting together the team to go to the Dominican Republic! It was a double confirmation, and by the end of the chapel I knew that I would be changing my summer plans. I had such an inner peace and excitement about the trip I knew it could only be from the Lord. So true Proverbs 16:9, which says,

"In their hearts humans plan their course,
but the Lord establishes their steps."

Marathon Madness

February 13, 1982

<u>STONE:</u>

God's strength to cross-country ski 20 miles for a fund raiser for the Dominican Republic when I was sick in bed.

It was February of 1982 and I was in the process of raising the $855 necessary to go to the Dominican Republic on a missions trip that May. A few team members decided to raise money by holding a 20-mile cross-country ski marathon around the back trails of Gordon College. I had sponsors who had pledged $150 and I was eager to ski. I knew it would be a challenge, but I was in shape and ready for it.

A few days before the marathon, I came down with a really bad cold and felt achy and was bed-ridden. I knew I wouldn't be able to do the whole marathon with the flu, but should I attempt to do just a few miles? I felt God encouraging me to try.

I did the first five mile loop in back of Coy Pond, and then I somehow did the same loop again to log ten miles. Although I was quite tired, I was amazed at how God had sustained me. Figuring I was done, I took off my skis and went to Lane Cafeteria for a hot chocolate. But then I felt like I should continue. When the twenty miles were done, I realized that it was only by God's strength and help that I had been able to finish the marathon. Zechariah 4:6 was true for me that day,

> *"Not by might nor by power,*
> *but by my Spirit,' says the Lord Almighty."*

Spared From Evil

August 3, 1982

STONE:

Closure with Becky Donaldson, my roommate, the night she died. "I'll see you at home later."

The whole Gordon campus was asking, "Why Becky?" Everyone was grieving the loss of such a special person who God had taken home the night before. Becky had been out running with Lotty, one of my four roommates, and she collapsed in her arms after completing her four mile run.

What amazed me was how God had prepared Becky to go home so unexpectedly. That very day, she had reconciled with her dad, she had settled important issues with her boyfriend, and she had special times with all her close friends. Right before her run, she came up to me while I was studying in the library and said, "I'll see you at home later." Little did she know how significant that statement would be for me, as just an hour later she would be entering her eternal home.

A few days after her death, her 20th birthday decorations were still hanging in our small apartment, and I was asking the Lord, "Why Becky?" I wasn't accusing the Lord of taking her, but just trying to understand the Lord's reason for taking her home so suddenly and so young. I picked up my Bible and started reading where I had left off the day before and came to Isaiah 57:1-2, which says,

> *"The righteous perish,*
> *and no one takes it to heart;*
> *the devout are taken away,*
> *and no one understands*
> *that the righteous are taken away*
> *to be spared from evil.*
> *Those who walk uprightly enter into peace;*
> *they find rest as they lie in death."*

God gave peace to my grieving heart. He wanted Becky home with Him and He had taken her in her beauty and gentleness and in the prime of her life in order to spare her from evil. He had prepared her to go home and He answered my questioning heart. He can be trusted.

Water in the Wilderness

May 25, 1983

STONE:

Interface hiking from Cascade Mountain to Owl's Head. Made it only halfway before dark. No water in that area but we prayed and Dan Murdock found some.

It was after my junior year that I participated in Gordon College's wilderness adventure camp called Interface. One day while in the Adirondacks, we had a really long and grueling climb up Cascade Mountain with 50 pound packs. We then went on toward Owl's Head, using a compass and bushwhacking. Night fell and we had to stop, but we were only halfway to our destination. We needed water for drinking and cooking but there wasn't any. We all came together and prayed, trusting God to meet our need or else to sustain us even without. We were all very thirsty.

While us campers put up tents and tarps in the dark, our leader Dan went off to see if he could find any water. He came back a little while later with water – the answer to our prayers.

Interestingly enough, the next day when we met up with Rich Obenchain, Interface's founder, he said that he had never seen any sign of water between Cascade Mountain and Owl's Head. And he had been leading groups in the area for many years. Hearing this made us all the more aware of God's hand in answering our prayer and providing what we needed.

Twelve Stones
Remembering the God Moments
by Laura Payne

As Steve mentioned in PEEKS, I am willing to share my own personal stories with you in the hope that you'll start recording God moments in your life in order to impact the next generation. As you read about the God moments in my life, perhaps they will motivate you to write down times in your own life when God has guided, protected, and blessed you. My desire with this book is to show how great and personal our God is, and my hope is that as you and I record the God moments, we can encourage the next generation to walk closer with Him.

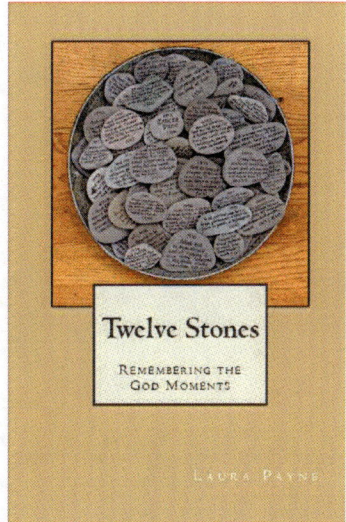

We are making the book available to you *at cost*. You can get a copy from me if you see me in person for $3.

Or you can order directly from Amazon at the following site. We've set the price at the minimum amount they allow:

> www.amazon.com/Twelve-Stones-Remembering-God-Moments/dp/1492352349/

If you prefer an e-book, you can download one for $0.99 at:

> www.amazon.com/Twelve-Stones-ebook/dp/B00FG7WXFC/

Camp Prayers

June 25 and July 1, 1984

STONE:

Camp kids and I pray for a job for me after summer camp. A call came from Gordon College for a tennis job when I never sought it.

The summer after I graduated from Gordon College, I worked at a Christian camp in New Hampshire called Brookwoods/Deer Run. I was the tennis instructor for the entire camp as well as a cabin counselor for twelve-year olds. Although at times it was a challenge to be in charge of the girls in my cabin, it was also a joy to see their simple faith as shown in their nightly prayers. They would pray for their dying pets, their family stresses, and their problems with boys.

One day I shared a prayer request with them. I asked, "Would you all pray that God would open up a job for me for after I finish working at this camp this summer?" We prayed about this for a few days. Then I got a note from the camp office that I had received a phone call from Steve Larson, the athletic director at Gordon College. I was supposed to call him back immediately.

Using the office phone, I returned his call and he offered me the head coaching position at Gordon College for both the men's and women's tennis teams. I was so excited! I asked him how he ever found out I was working at the camp in order to call me. He said that he had called my parents to get the information.

This job offer, which of course I accepted, was a total surprise to me, but not to God who had orchestrated Steve's call in response to our prayers. The kids in my cabin were amazed at how God answered their request, and it helped build all of us up in our faith in Him.

Heart Transformation

May 16, 1985

God changing my heart from missions being the last thing I ever wanted to do (Pilgrim Baptist as a kid) to it being the desire of my heart.

When I was young, I attended Pilgrim Baptist Church in Glastonbury. A few times a year there were missionaries that would come to speak. They always looked so old-fashioned with their horn-rimmed glasses and out-of-style clothes which they had probably picked up at a thrift store. And their stories always had to do with primitive living conditions. I used to think to myself, "The last thing I ever want to be is a missionary." Not only did the missionaries stick out like sore thumbs, but I couldn't imagine raising a family in such remote, dangerous places as the locations they described.

But God TOTALLY transformed my heart over the years to the point that by the time I was 23 years old, being a missionary was what I wanted *most* to be! How was this possible? God just kept putting His desires in my heart – desires for Him, for His Word, and then for those who wouldn't have a chance to hear about Him if ordinary people like myself didn't go and bring them His Word. I knew there were only two things that are lasting in this life (people's souls and the Word of God), so what better way could there be to spend my time here on earth than in bringing God's Word to those who need it most?

God transformed my heart. What greater miracle could there be than that?

12

Puppy Love

June 18, 1985

STONE:

God answered my prayer to know His love more through two men beating a puppy with clubs in Pasadena, California, instead of me.

When I was 23 years old, God led me to go on a short-term missions trip to Pakistan with Frontiers Mission. Before the trip I sent out a newsletter, and one of the prayer requests was that God would help me understand more of His love for me during that summer.

A few weeks later, I was at the training phase of the trip in Pasadena, California. One evening around midnight, I was walking alone back to my dorm after doing laundry, when two African American men came around a corner. They held wooden clubs and started to beat a young puppy. They looked up at me for a moment. I felt like they were wondering if I'd be the better "prey" to attack. Then they focused their maliciousness back on the puppy, making fun of it and beating it until it was hardly moving. The puppy looked my direction, helpless, innocent, taking a beating it didn't deserve, and one that was possibly in my place. If the puppy hadn't been there, I could have been the one being beaten and dying.

I ran back to my dorm, lay down on my bed and wept. My tears were not the result of fear, although I'm sure I had some adrenaline rushing though my veins. No, it was because I now had such a graphic physical demonstration of just how much God loved me. He voluntarily was mocked and beaten, as that puppy had been, so that I wouldn't have to suffer death myself. He loved me so much as to take the punishment I deserved so that I could have life – eternal life – with Him. What amazing love He has for me!

God answered my prayer for wanting to know His love for me in such a demonstrative way that it's engraved on my heart and mind forever.

The Wrong Path

July 14, 1985

STONE:

Angel appears to a Pakistani and tells him, "You are on the wrong path. Jesus is coming soon." Happened twice. He came to church.

The summer of 1985, I was on a short-term missions trip to Karachi, Pakistan. One evening, a member of our group spoke at a church service in an old but beautiful church building. Only 15 people showed up besides those in our group. Muslim children were playing just outside the window, and Muslim men and women were walking by the door. Inside we joined the few believers in singing antiquated hymns that sounded almost like funeral dirges to my heart. During the message, the mosque's call to worship drowned out the speaker's voice. "What kind of bondage are these people in, Lord?" I asked myself. "Why is the church so dead? Why do the millions perish without knowing that You died for their sins?" I later wrote these questions in my journal as I remembered experiencing that moment.

After the church service was over, a Pakistani man can up to two of our leaders and told them why he was there that night. He said that on his way to the mosque that evening, an old man told him that he was going on the wrong path. The Pakistani man proceeded on his way and went to the mosque anyway. However, on the way back from the mosque, he saw the old man again and once again was told, "You are on the wrong path." He then added, "Jesus is coming soon." Immediately after saying this, the old man suddenly disappeared from his view. The Pakistani man was so startled by this that he came to the church to find out more about Jesus and about Jesus' path.

How amazing God is to call people to Himself who might not otherwise seek Him or even have a chance to know Him! God is good!

Bowing in Worship

August 10, 1985

STONE:

Crazy Pakistani wielding knife bows down and acknowledges God when we sang the song, "I Exalt Thee." (Revelation 3:9)

Before I went to Pakistan the summer of 1985, God encouraged me that the words of Revelation 3:7-9 were for my time there. They say,

> *"These are the words of him who is holy and true, who holds the key of David. What he opens no one can shut, and what he shuts no one can open. I know your deeds. See, I have placed before you an open door that no one can shut. I know that you have little strength, yet you have kept my word and have not denied my name. I will make those who are of the synagogue of Satan, who claim to be Jews though they are not, but are liars – I will make them come and fall down at your feet and acknowledge that I have loved you."*

That summer while our team was in Pakistan, a man did fall at our feet, bowing in worship as we worshipped Jesus. Here is what I wrote in my journal concerning this – one of our last days in Pakistan. It was written after a "Joshua Walk," which is a walk around part of the city during which we pray as we walk and silently sing praise songs, asking God to spiritually awaken people to know Him.

"Today was our last Joshua Walk and we walked for two hours in the morning. We had a choice where we wanted to go and since I had missed the first walk in Lyari, I went there with Ted, Ruth and Dan. We walked and prayed in twos (Ted and I) and it was a good time to envision God's work there, praying especially for Noor and her household.

When we were near the end of our Joshua Walk, an old man started following us (he sounded and looked like Popeye), grumbling to himself in his Popeye voice and every once in a while making outbursts to people around him. After a while he was walking right next to us, picking up rocks along the way and throwing them over walls, over curtain dividers of houses, and to the sides of the road. He turned over jagged sewer covers and exposed the smells and garbage underneath. He tore crumpled papers out of mud and rock walls and left them on the ground.

As he moved ahead of Ted and me, I started praying for him to understand that the Lord could save him. As we walked on, he kept looking back over his shoulder to see where we were going. A thin pocket knife appeared in his right hand which he kept partly hidden by the dirty brown sleeve of his cuff. Ted then prayed for God's protection, thanking Him for His sovereign control over the situation.

We continued to walk behind our unelected guide who cleared our way by throwing rocks and making children scurry out of the streets with his grumbling. He was, or seemed to be, the reproach of the area – a man in his 70's or 80's, short grayed hair in a crew-cut style, prickly white scruff on his wrinkled face, and eyes which were dark and worn. He moved as though he resented every step. He looked as though neither he nor his clothes had seen clean water in months. Where was his family? Was there no one to take care of him?

As a group (Ruth, Ted, Dan and I), we decided to sit down, sing some songs and have some water. The Popeye man sat a few feet away on the rock step of a home. We sang 2-3 songs, then sang the song with the chorus, "We exalt Thee, we exalt Thee, we exalt Thee, Oh Lord…" As soon as we got to the first chorus of "We exalt Thee," the man got down on his hands and knees right in front of us and bowed to the ground as

Muslims pray, facing away from us. He bowed in reverence around 5 or 6 times, each time turning a bit, so that on the last bow he was facing us.

After we finished the song (quieting down a little in the middle due to our amazement, but then louder at the end), he got up and sat down next to Dan. They talked (or tried to communicate for a while) and then we all split up.

I thought a lot about what took place and about this man. He is the lowest in his society, and yet he praised the one, true God. How did he know what we were singing? Oh Father, so often, I do not understand Your greatness, holiness and power. The vilest offenders can't help but praise Your name. It reminds me of the verses in Philippians 2:9-11,

"Therefore God exalted him to the highest place
and gave him the name
that is above every name,
that at the name of Jesus every knee should bow,
in heaven and on earth and under the earth,
and every tongue acknowledge that Jesus Christ
is Lord, to the glory of God the Father."

For a Future Generation

May 20, 1986

STONE:

Call to Wycliffe Bible Translators at Quest (1 Peter 1:24-25) and confirmation (Psalm 102:18).

After college, I coached and taught tennis during the academic school year. I had the option to keep teaching in the summer, but wanted to use that time to try to determine God's direction for my life. The summer of 1985 in Pakistan clarified for me that God had given me a call to missions. Now it was the summer of 1986 and I was praying that God would guide me specifically in one of two ways: either using my teaching and athletic skills overseas as a "tent maker," or confirm that I should go into Bible translation work. So I decided to divide my summer, first going to Wycliffe's orientation program for Bible translation in Canada, and second taking courses at the Samuel Zweymer Institute in Pasadena, California. There I would volunteer at the Center for World Missions where I could try to find a tent-making opportunity in a Muslim country.

So in May, I drove to Canada for a three-week long course, which immersed me into what it would be like to be involved in Bible translation work. My heart was being pulled toward this work even though I was not particularly good at language learning. I just knew that God's Word was a lifeline between Him and myself, and I couldn't imagine anyone not having the chance to hear it. Not only that, but I knew that if I went as a missionary somewhere, I might influence a few people for the Lord in my years among them, but the impact wouldn't be as lasting as if I left them the Word of God in their mother tongue.

My heart was telling me that Bible translation work was what I should do, but my mind was telling me it was ridiculous since languages were my worst subject in school, so I spent a morning alone with the Lord, asking Him what I should do. I went to a basement classroom where I could be alone and I had my journal and Bible in hand. I asked God to lead me. I looked around the room and it was pretty bare. But there was one word written in big letters on the blackboard: PETER. When I saw this, I thought, "Okay, Lord, I'll just start reading in Peter." When I got to the end of 1 Peter 1, my jaw dropped in amazement. My question as to what I should do in missions disappeared as I read the words in verses 24-25:

> *"All people are like grass,*
> *and all their glory is like the flowers of the field; the*
> *grass withers and the flowers fall,*
> *but the word of the Lord endures forever."*

My "glory" was in my athletic ability. That would pass away over time like the flowers and grass of the field. But the Word of the Lord would stand forever, long after I would leave wherever it was that God would call me to work.

I left that basement classroom encouraged to join Wycliffe, but the next day my brain kicked in and said, "You've got to be kidding if you think you can do this work! You need more confirmation than just this one verse!" So that afternoon I begged the Lord to pardon my unbelief, but that I needed yet one more sign to know this was the course He was choosing for my life. I don't do this often, and especially not for guidance, but that time I just flipped open the Bible and asked Him to guide my reading yet one more time. The page opened to Psalm 102, and in verse 18 I read,

> *"Let this be written for a future generation,*
> *that a people not yet created*
> *may praise the Lord."*

God is amazing, meeting us on our path and causing our humanness to collide with His almighty plans.

The Wedding Ring

Fall 1987

STONE:

Steve left his wedding ring on top of the car by mistake. We went for a ride on a bumpy dirt road for a half hour. The ring was still there later!

S teve and I had only been married a month or so when we moved to an apartment complex right across from College of the Siskiyous. One of our first weeks there, we took a ride in our "Green Machine" on some dirt roads that were quite bumpy, just to see the area.

When we got back to our apartment, I noticed that Steve wasn't wearing his wedding ring. I was surprised and asked him where it was. He responded in shock as he realized that right before our car ride, he had worked on the engine, placing his ring on top of the car so it wouldn't get caught on something while he was working.

We thought the ring must now be long gone, but hoping beyond hope, Steve ran down to the car to take a look. And there on top of the roof was his gold wedding band! God miraculously kept it there, much to our unbelief and anxious hearts.

Amazing how God will go to extremes in spite of us to show us His great love and presence in our lives.

An Unexpected Explosion

September 1988

STONE:

God protected me from a gas stove that blew up with me only a few feet away from it.

Every summer my parents lease a rustic cabin on a lake in Maine. It used to be part of a girls' camp where my mom went when she was a teenager. I can only remember a few times in my life when I wasn't able to spend some part of a summer there on vacation.

After Steve and I moved back to the East Coast to raise support for going overseas, we decided to spend a week in Maine to enjoy some peace at the lake. We had the cabin all to ourselves, which was a rare occurrence as we usually had to share it with my parents and brother.

My mom usually cooks when we are at the cabin, but with just Steve and I there, I had to try and remember how to light the gas stove. I knew my mom always opened the oven door, lit a match and placed it down a hole where it would ignite the gas. I followed suit and then closed the oven door.

I continued preparing the meal in the kitchen when all of a sudden there was a huge blast that sounded like a canon accompanied by a ball of fire. I was only a few feet away from the oven door as it blew open, and the explosion threw me into the living room. The kitchen windows blew out and glass rained down everywhere. Steve was on the couch in the living room, looking wide-eyed at me. Amazingly, I was still standing, I had absolutely no cuts, and the fireball had not singed me at all.

After comprehending the magnitude of what had just happened, I went up the hill to talk with the owner of the camp. I asked him if he had heard anything unusual. He said he heard what he thought was a canon going off across the lake. I told him it had been the oven in our cabin and apologized profusely for my lack of oven-lighting expertise! He assured me it wasn't my fault, that the oven was old and needed to be replaced. He was just relieved that I wasn't hurt.

I know that God's hands or those of His mighty angels were protecting me during that explosion. Only by His watchful care could I have emerged from that kitchen unscathed.

Closed Doors

November 7, 1988

STONE:

God closing the door to Nepal and Asia and confirming Senegal to both Steve and me. Greatest need, small SIL branch. Two confirmations: French book and mail missions newsletter.

After Steve and I got married in 1987, we started raising support to go to the "closed" country of Nepal with Wycliffe Bible Translators. However after ten months of raising support, our visas fell through with no sign of it changing in the near future. We checked out other Asian countries but in each case we were met by closed doors. We both decided it was time to turn our eyes toward Africa.

After individually reading all the profiles of the African countries that Wycliffe was working in, we sat down together and discovered we were both being drawn to Senegal. I then told the Lord, "I want to make sure that my desire to serve in Senegal is Your desire, Lord. Confirm it this week by bringing up Senegal in different situations and NOT other African countries."

That week there were two confirmations. The first was when I opened my old French book to the next lesson that Steve and I were going over together and the chapter was devoted to the country of Senegal. I flipped through the book and saw that it was the ONLY African country covered in the entire book. The second confirmation was receiving a missions newsletter a few days later that had "SENEGAL" written in big letters across the front page. There was no other mail that week with any mention of any other African country.

God had put His will for us in our hearts, and He led us as we sought to follow Him. He confirmed this leading very clearly so that in the future when things got hard in Senegal, we would stay the course and finish the work to which He had called us.

Back Problems

August 16, 1989

STONE:

Steve had lower back problems for 3 ½ weeks. Prayed and he was miraculously up the whole day his folks arrived in Paris and thereafter.

Steve and I were in language study in France in 1989 when he hurt his back and couldn't sit or stand for more than an hour at a time. He had to spend his days in bed nursing the inflamed nerve in his lower back. The doctor said to just "rest". We prayed a lot that week, knowing that his folks would be coming to France to visit us the first day of the following week. At that point, the problem had been going on for almost a month.

No real improvement occurred and it was the day to take the train to Paris to greet his parents. We prayed there would be a place on the journey to rest, and God provided us with the back seats on the train – two seats for Steve to stretch out on. This was amazing as the TGV was very full! We arrived in Paris the night before Steve's parents so he rested that whole evening.

The next morning we woke up early to go to the airport, taking time to pray for strength for Steve's back to make it through a LONG day of traveling. Steve was up almost the whole day and said he was absolutely amazed. To go in one day from having to be in bed most of the day, to the next where he was able to be up most of the day, was really a miracle.

From that day on, Steve's back started progressively getting better, to the point where at the end of the trip he could carry his daypack into the mountains of Switzerland. As Isaiah 40:31 says,

> *"But those who hope in the Lord*
> *will renew their strength.*
> *They will soar on wings like eagles;*

they will run and not grow weary,
they will walk and not be faint."

The Rapture

1990

STONE:

*Two dreams of being raptured near Faneuil Hall in Boston.
Later Steve tells me of a dream he had before mine of him
being raptured from Park Street Church 1 mile away.*

When I was studying French in Besancon, France, I had
the same dream two nights in a row. I was walking on a
plaza right near the steps leading down to Faneuil Hall in
Boston when all of a sudden I was raptured up into the sky. It
was the most freeing and joyful feeling I've ever experienced.
Each time, as soon I was raptured, I woke up. I never told
Steve about these dreams.

One evening a few years later, Steve and I were sitting in
Roger and Dawn Johnson's living room in front of their
fireplace catching up with them. For some reason the subject
of the rapture came up. Steve told us of a dream that he had
before he met me – one of being raptured from the Park Street
Church in Boston. He also had felt that indescribable, freeing
sensation and joy as he rose into the sky. I then asked him how
he knew it was that church as he had never been to Boston
before meeting me. He said he had only heard of the church
because they are very missions minded, but that somehow he
just knew that he was in that church. I then told him of my two
dreams back when I was in France. The places of our raptures
were less than a mile apart!

This was such an encouragement to us to know that God
had spoken to our hearts each individually about the same
future event. Now every time we are together in Boston, the
possibility of going home certainly crosses our minds! ☺

Praying for Missionaries

May 3, 1991

STONE:

God led us to work in Diembering: village dancing welcome, prayer of elders (10 year wait/tears), small house open for us, people desiring God's word in Kwatay.

In May of 1991, we drove down to the Casamance to check out three language allocations that the SIL Senegal branch had proposed to us as possible sites for us to do translation. The first day we checked out Oussouye, but it was clear to us from the church's tepid welcome and their past history working with other missionaries that we were not to work there. The next day we drove out to Diembering to check out the situation with the Kwatay people. As we approached the town, we were met by crowds of people in brightly-colored outfits singing, dancing, and waving, seemingly to greet us. We were amazed at the welcome – and only later heard that we had come in just moments behind the governor's convoy as he was entering the village!

We talked to the elders of the church, who with great emotion and tears in their eyes told us that for the last ten years they had been praying for a missionary to come! What an encouragement and affirmation that was to us. They also said that for years now the few people in the church had been coming on Sundays just to pray, since their French was so limited they couldn't read the French Bible. When we told them we hoped to help bring God's Word to them in their own language, Kwatay, they were very excited.

After the amazing welcome and the need expressed, my heart was confident that this was the place for us. Now we just needed to find a place to live in the village. Ouffi, a Kwatay believer who was showing us around his village, couldn't think of any vacant houses where we could stay. So we prayed for wisdom. As we toured the village, we saw a very small cement-block home on top of a hill overlooking the ocean that seemed

27

abandoned. We asked Ouffi about it and he said that it used to belong to a foreigner doing oil excavation work in the area, but now it was owned by the community. He said we could ask the community leaders if we could rent it out. Amazingly it worked out, all in that one day!

God's guidance was clear that we were to live and work in Diembering with the Kwatay.

Knee Surgery Blessings

July 28, 1991

STONE:

Paul, our language helper, had to work in the rice fields. The afternoon he told us we prayed, and God brought Augustin (who couldn't work in the fields because of a knee surgery).

We had moved into our small house on the hill in Diembering and had just started trying to learn Kwatay when our language helper, Paul Diatta, said he had to stop working with us to go work in the rice fields with his family. Paul said that at this time of the year it would be impossible to find someone to help us who knew both French and Kwatay since any of the young men who had studied French at school were needed in the fields for the rice cultivation season.

After Paul left, Steve and I prayed that God would provide someone to help us learn the language. That afternoon, a young man named Augustin was slowly walking by our home and we greeted him. We invited him up on our porch to talk and he asked what we were doing in his village. We told him about our hopes to learn his language and then in the future to help translate the Bible into it. We asked if he knew of anyone who could help us learn his language. He said that he could. He had just arrived back in the village after having knee surgery and wouldn't be able to work in the rice fields that summer.

God answered our prayers that same day with what Paul thought would be an impossibility. God showed us once again that with Him all things are possible!

Called by Name

November 21, 1991

<u>STONE:</u>

Awoken at 2:30 a.m. by an audible voice so near that it was almost a whisper, "Laura".

We had been in living in Diembering for six months when one night I was awoken by a soft-spoken voice near my head saying my name, "Laura." I immediately woke up, as did Steve. I asked him if he had said my name but he said no. I actually didn't think it was him because it didn't sound like him, but who else could have been there, whispering my name? We discussed that it couldn't have been a Kwatay speaker as they have a thick accent when they pronounce my name. Steve even got up and went to the door to see if anyone was outside, but no one was there. There was no one but us and God.

Steve got back in under the mosquito net, lay down on our mattress on the floor and was soon asleep. I lay there beside him saying, "Speak, Lord, for Your servant is listening…"

Although I didn't hear that small, audible voice again that night or any other night since then, it makes me know that God is so very close to us – just a whisper away. What an encouragement it was to know His presence was with us at the very beginning of our work among the Kwatay!

The Gift of Life

February 28, 1992

STONE:

Steve's 30th birthday, almost losing Nika (tonsillitis). Prayers of people, medicine kicked in.

People say that the day you turn 30 years old is a big day. For Steve it was a day we will never forget. Nika, who was not quite one year old, had been very sick the entire week with high fevers and weight loss. By the end of the week she couldn't eat or drink. We tried giving her two different kinds of malaria medicine, and then started her on a course of antibiotics after seeing a doctor in Cap Skirring who thought she had tonsillitis and not malaria. But the day after seeing the doctor she was worse to the point where she just lay whimpering and listless in our arms, almost comatose. That day was Steve's 30th birthday.

Steve walked up a sandy hill by our village to plead with God to give us back our only child. During his walk, he felt impressed he needed to call the SIL director in Dakar. He finally got through to him right before his money at the pay phone ran out, and just had enough time to tell him to pray for Nika, because unless God intervened that day we were afraid we were going to lose her.

We drove back to Cap Skirring to see the doctor and show him our little girl. There was a plane on the tarmac which we could see from his office, and we told him we would find a way to get on that plane if getting to Dakar would save our daughter. He reassured us that the antibiotic would soon start to work, that it hadn't quite been 24 hours since she had started taking it.

By faith we drove the bumpy dirt road back to our village. As we were going, Nika started to show a small interest in nursing again after days of refusing. By the time we reached the village, she had life back in her eyes and she could sit up on her own again.

31

We called the SIL director back and told him that Nika seemed to have turned a corner and was now getting better. He said that in the two hours since our call, he had gathered the whole Senegal branch together to pray for her. So we all praised God together for His direct answer to our concerted prayers.

The next day Nika was on the road to recovery, eating, walking and playing once again. What relief and joy we felt at having Nika given back to us, as if from the dead. This is how Abraham must have felt upon getting his son Isaac back off the altar. As it says in Genesis 22:14,

"On the mountain of the Lord it will be provided."

From Seed to Fruit

June 7, 1992

STONE:

First time singing praise songs in Kwatay. Alistair said, "Many years ago a seed was planted here. Now we are seeing its growth."

We had been living in Diembering for a year, learning the Kwatay language and culture, when we asked our translator William if he would attempt to translate some songs into his language. He said that his people had never sung in their mother tongue because they thought it was too "heavy" – it just didn't sound good. So all their songs were in Diola Kasa. We encouraged him to give it a try with the hope that the songs would speak to the people's hearts more than singing in a second language. So he worked on it and translated a number of worship songs from Kasa and French into Kwatay.

We then made a songbook, printed it in Dakar, and brought the books back down to the village to see what the Christians in our small church would think. We presented the books at the beginning of the service, thanking William for all his hard work. After passing out the books, we all started to sing. Not long after, old Edward burst out with a first-time ever, "Alleluia!" After the song finished, another elder, Alistair, said something like this:

"Many years ago, the first missionaries came and a seed was planted here in Diembering. But now, with these songs in our language, we are seeing its fruit."

Singing God's praise in the heart language really does make all the difference. It was such a confirmation to Steve and I to press on to help them have God's Word in their mother tongue, because we saw how much it could speak to their hearts.

Razor-Sharp Machetes

July 11, 1992

STONE:

Circumcision ceremony where God stopped the men from proudly displaying the spirits' protection. The head Animist got mad at me.

We never witnessed a more overt power struggle between God and the spirits of darkness than occurred one day in July, 1992. It took place the day after we returned to Diembering, after attending the SIL Senegal Branch's spiritual retreat, which was focused that year on spiritual warfare. Talk about God's perfect timing! When we arrived in the village, there was a circumcision celebration going on. It was the first one in a Kwatay village in over 20 years, and people had come from all over the region.

All the people were gathered together in one of the town squares to sing, dance and see the power of the fetishes and gris-gris. This power was demonstrated in several ways, but the most impressive was when some of the dancing men took sharp knives and tried to cut themselves.

Our first day back in the village, Steve went out and took some video of what was happening. When he returned home he told me that men were taking razor-sharp machetes (which they showed could easily slice through a mango), and they sawed them back and forth across their arms, legs and even their mouths. The libations they poured out to the spirits and the gris-gris they were wearing protected them from being cut, so they weren't hurt at all as they displayed the spirits' power. Steve said he'd take care of Nika after church the next day so that I could go and see it for myself.

When I arrived on the scene the following day, there was a large crowd of over 500 people circled around a number of men covered with amulets and gris-gris. The men were singing, dancing, and chanting in the middle of the mob, and pouring out libations to the spirits. One man strutted forward and in a grand display he poured some type of liquid over his body. He proudly waved his machete in front of him, confident in the spirits' power to keep him safe from the sharp blade. God's Spirit tore at my heart and I thought, "Satan can't have this victory – not this time." I started to pray, "Lord, don't let the powers of darkness confer any power to this man. Even if it means he will die from cutting himself with his machete, let it so be. And if You want to show Yourself stronger than the spirits and heal him in Jesus' name, I am here as Your servant. Crush the enemy, Lord. Crush the enemy."

I stayed for an hour – praying continually. I was exhausted but knew I had to continue. I couldn't stop. God was confounding the ranks of the enemy and the fetishers seemed to sense it. The man who was haughtily waving his machete went over to talk with the other influential men. They seemed confused. Sensing that God was answering my prayers, I asked a lady standing next to me why the man hadn't tried to cut himself yet. She said she had no idea. Every other time he had always demonstrated the power of the spirits. Then the whole dance ceremony broke up and people started going en masse toward another neighborhood in our village. I asked someone else what was happening and he said they were going to change locations and dance at one of the other town squares.

I knew that I couldn't go home. I had to keep up the battle, so I tagged along with the crowd. But as I was walking, the man who had been strutting and pouring libations on his body came up to me and waved his finger in my face, speaking harshly to me in a language I didn't understand. He was very irritated. Then he left me and kept going. This confirmed what I already knew, that God was answering my prayer and removing the spirits' protection from these men. They knew that if they tried to cut themselves without the spirits' power, they would, and so they didn't dare try.

I continued following the crowd to the next location. Once again the fetishers started dancing and chanting, wielding their machetes in a proud display. I continued to pray, "Crush the enemy, Lord. Confuse the enemy. Send Your angels to fight this battle." Once again the older men seemed confused and they started quarreling with one another. I kept praying. After 30 minutes in the new location, they abandoned the dance. Food started to arrive and everyone sat down to eat. I then went home.

God had won a victory. He had displayed His power, which was greater than the enemies. And God's servant was exhausted. I never did get to see for myself the men trying to cut themselves that Sunday afternoon, but I saw it later on the video footage which Steve had taken. You could actually see the spirits' control in the eyes of the men who were strutting and dancing.

God taught us a powerful lesson through that experience – that if we would pray, He would show Himself stronger than the powers of darkness. This became the theme of our message at churches as we went home not long after for our first furlough. And many joined in to pray for the Kwatay, that God would bring them from centuries of darkness to the light of His Word.

Five Year Mark

October 17, 1992

STONE:

Marriage confirmation on our 5th anniversary. "The Lord will create a new thing on earth – a woman will surround a man." Jeremiah 31:22 in my One Year Bible reading.

We celebrated our fifth wedding anniversary in Diembering. Steve and Nika went for a walk through the fields and brought back some flowers in a cup for me. While they were gone, I made Steve's favorite dessert – chocolate brownies with mint frosting. I blew up and hung five balloons, one for each year, and put numbers on them. I also placed a card I had written the day before on the kitchen table. We then ate brownies and played cribbage. It was simple but meaningful.

But what stands out most to me from that five-year mark together was what happened that evening. I was having my quiet time under our mosquito net before bed, reading that day's entry in my One Year Bible, and Jeremiah 31:22 jumped out at me. It says,

> *"The Lord will create a new thing on earth –*
> *a woman will surround a man."*

I was amazed to read those words on my fifth anniversary. God had used that exact verse years before when I was single and had been thinking of dating someone else. He used it to speak to my heart that I was not to date that guy, but that He would bring along one in the future who was to be my husband.

A few years later when I met Steve, I felt freedom from the Lord to date him, and eventually to marry him. But I never had an outright confirmation from the Lord that Steve was "the one" which He had told me about earlier. So when times were hard, as they often are in marriage, I wondered to myself if I had made the right decision. Now it was our fifth anniversary and God gave me a late, but very clear confirmation, that Steve was the one He intended for me.

It never ceases to amaze me how God uses His Word to speak clearly to us in our specific situations.

Last Minute Evacuation

October 31, 1992

STONE:

Hard first year and a half in Diembering. Evacuated due to rebel killings. But God gave a confirmation verse (Psalm 102:18) in my daily reading to encourage me that we are in His will.

Two months before our first furlough, Diola rebels started killing people in the Casamance who were not from their ethnic group. They mainly targeted Wolofs and Senegalese from the north, but expatriates were also caught in the crossfire. One day the entire Serer fishing village down the road from us in Cap Skirring was burned to the ground with 31 dead. The SIL Director called us and said he wanted us out of the region immediately. Since we had to gather our belongings for our upcoming furlough and close up our house, he reluctantly allowed us 24 hours to pack up and leave.

We left early the next afternoon, hoping the rebels wouldn't be out on the roads in the heat of the day. Our translator William and others from the church prayed us off. As we headed down the road, there were people fleeing, carrying all their possessions on their backs. Cars and trucks were turned over in ditches. Some had been burned, others had been sprayed with bullets. We made it safely to Ziguinchor, a zone of relative peace. The dangerous part of our journey was over.

That night I read the chapters in my "Daily Walk through the Bible", and I came to a verse that God used six years previously to confirm that I was to go into Bible translation work, Psalm 102:18:

> *"Let this be written for a future generation,*
> *that a people not yet created*
> *may praise the Lord."*

God wanted me to know that His plan and purpose for what we were doing had not changed, even in the midst of chaos and uprising. He wanted to once again confirm His calling to us: to bring His Word to those in Diembering.

Frozen Chicken

1993

STONE:

God protected me by deflecting the tip of a sharp knife away from my left eye.

We were on furlough and staying with the Johnson's at their beautiful home in Lake Shastina, California. One afternoon I realized that I hadn't planned anything for dinner. There was some frozen chicken in the freezer, so I took it out, hoping it would thaw before I had to cook it a few hours later.

Unfortunately the chicken still seemed frozen solid as dinnertime approached. I took a sharp cutting knife out of the drawer and wedged the tip between the frozen thighs. It wouldn't budge so I applied more force. All of a sudden, I felt something so close to my left eye that there was a brush of air against my eyeball. Then I heard the sound of metal hitting the floor to my left. It was the tip of the sharp knife!

God watched over me and protected me that day. Was the wisp of air against my eye an angel's wing batting that sharp tip away? Someday I'll know!

Out of the Womb

September 6, 1993

<u>STONE:</u>

*God gave me Psalm 22:9-10 the night before Kevin was born,
giving me peace for the birth, and that this child would be His.*

During the last months of our first furlough we were living
at Gordon-Conwell Theological Seminary where Steve
was taking some Greek classes, and I was due to give birth to
our second child. I came down with a cold a few days before
my due date, so I prayed the baby would come late so that I'd
have the strength to give birth naturally, as I'd done with Nika.
God granted my request. A week after my due date, I was
walking around the rolling campus hills with my mom, and I
told her I thought I was well enough now to give birth. Still,
the vivid memories of Nika's difficult delivery made me fearful
that I wouldn't have the strength to do it again naturally.

That night I went into labor. It was around 8 p.m. when the
contractions started. We watched a movie which helped pass
the time during the early stages of labor. After the movie I
grabbed my Bible to have a quiet time before trying to get a
few hours of rest until the intense contractions would make
rest impossible. I randomly opened to the Psalms and read
Psalm 22:9-10:

> *"Yet you brought me out of the womb;*
> *you made me trust in you*
> *even at my mother's breast.*
> *From birth I was cast on you;*
> *from my mother's womb*
> *you have been my God."*

When I read this my anxious thoughts disappeared and my
heart was at peace. Not only would God get me through this
birth so that I would hold my baby close to my breast, but God
was giving me the confirmation that this child would be His.
Now my heart was full of praise and joy as I went into the

night of contractions and labor, because the promise of God was before me.

Kevin Andrew Payne came into the world at 8:35 a.m. the next morning, on Labor Day no less! I thank God for using His Word to speak to me, as the song says,

> *"He walks with me and He talks with me,*
> *along life's narrow ways…"*

Indeed He lives, and I could now praise Him yet again for the new life He had given us.

The Aqua Shirt

February 5, 1995

STONE:

I had two dreams/visions of Kevin falling into our well and dying. I prayed. The next day Kevin dressed in the same outfit as in my dream. God warned us in advance and protected him.

Our family was in the village in Senegal and Kevin was two and a half years old. One night I woke up after having a dream or vision of Kevin falling into our well and drowning. I prayed and tried to go back to sleep. But once again I was hit with the vivid picture of Kevin on the wall of our well just about to fall in. I wrestled on my bed for an hour and a half, praying for God's protection over my little boy and that my heart wouldn't give way to fear. Finally peace came and I fell asleep. In the morning I mentioned to Steve that I didn't sleep well due to a dream I had (I wasn't really asleep or awake – it seemed more like a vision, since it was as clear as day).

Later in the morning, I got Kevin into his clothes for church, pulling his aqua shirt over his head. A flashback came to me that this was the exact shirt he was wearing in my vision the night before. For the first time that morning I realized that the vision I had seen was actually a warning to me about that very day! From that moment on I kept a close eye on Kevin and made sure he was near me as much as possible.

In the afternoon some disgruntled men came into our courtyard, very agitated and angry. Kevin was playing in the sandbox, not far from our well where the men were standing. I immediately picked him up and brought him inside our mud brick home. I felt in my heart that this was what my warning was for. They were disputing over the boundary lines of the mission house's property, and in their culture land is a very serious business. Steve called our translator William over, and they got out the deed to our land and showed it to the men so that they could see for themselves the written contract signed by their own people. The men went away somewhat appeased.

I praised God the rest of the day that He gave me not only a warning to protect Kevin from harm's way, but that He also opened my eyes to see it when it came. He truly loves and watches over us in amazing ways!

Live Through Me

April 6, 1995

STONE:

God immediately healed my heart and lungs when I asked Jesus to live through me after Nika was sick for three weeks.

When Nika was four years old, she was sick in the village with what we thought was malaria, and it persisted for three weeks despite four different malaria treatments. As she got worse and worse we made the decision to evacuate her to Dakar to get further tests and blood work done. When we arrived, we found out that in addition to malaria she also had tonsillitis and needed a course of antibiotics.

I had been so worried about Nika that my heart and lungs had gradually gotten tighter and more painful to the point where I couldn't find a comfortable position to rest. It hurt both to breathe in and to exhale. At that point I thought I might die! I lay down on my bed to read the Word, confess my sins, and beseech the Lord for mercy for not only Nika, but now for my very own life. "Please don't take my life now, Lord. My kids really need me."

Then it was as if God was talking to me and He replied, "They don't need you, Laura. What they need is Me living in you." Instantly I knew that the Lord was right and I laid down my life once again and asked Him to be my very life and to live through me, His servant.

As soon as I finished that prayer, God instantly healed me, taking away all the pain in my heart and lungs. I rose from the bed astonished that there was not even a hint of residual pain in my chest. Praising the Lord, I went out renewed in His strength and in His Spirit to serve my kids.

A Cargo of Mangoes

August, 1995

STONE:

God protected our family from being on the Joola ferry by filling the hold with mangoes so we couldn't fit our car on board, saving us from a violent storm.

While we were living in the Southern Casamance region of Senegal, translating the New Testament for the Kwatay people, we often needed to make trips up to the capital city of Dakar in the North where our SIL center was located. It was a grueling and hot ten-hour drive by car over roads filled with potholes and check points. So most trips we opted to drive two hours to the town of Ziguinchor where we could board our car on a large ferry and rent a small sleeping berth for a more restful, overnight trip up to the capital.

On one journey during the rainy season in August, we had planned to take the Joola ferry. We purchased tickets for both our vehicle and a sleeping berth in advance, so that when we got there the day of the voyage we wouldn't have to worry about the ferry being sold out.

When the day arrived, we drove out from our village, arriving in Ziguinchor in plenty of time to load our car onto the ship. Crowds of people and produce filled the boarding area, and as we looked into the hold, we couldn't believe our eyes. The place where cars were supposed to park was piled fifteen-feet high with mangoes! We went to the ticket counter to ask how they were planning to fit our car on board. They said there was no way, and that we'd just have to leave it in Ziguinchor, or drive up to Dakar. We knew we couldn't just leave our packed vehicle in the South for a month, so we grudgingly accepted a refund and stayed that night with missionary friends in Ziguinchor.

In the middle of the night I woke to thunder, violent winds and torrential rain that lasted for some time. My mind went directly to the ferry that was still on the ocean, making its way up the coast to Dakar. Our translator, William, was on board so I prayed for him and the boat's safety during the storm.

The next morning, we woke up early and made the long drive up North in relentless heat. Kevin was sick so I coddled him in the back seat. It was hard to be thankful on the car ride, when if we had just been able to board the ferry with the ticket we'd bought in advance, we'd have already been at our destination, cool and refreshed. We arrived late that night in Dakar, exhausted but happy to finally be able to just crash in one of the apartments at the SIL center.

The next day, our translator William came to the center to work with us. He told us that two nights before, when he had been at sea on the Joola, a large storm suddenly came up at 2:00 a.m. The ferry was tossed by huge waves and the mangoes in the hold shifted to one side, causing the ship to tilt precariously on its side. Life jackets were passed out to those on the top deck, but there were not enough for the 2,000 people on board. As people below deck started to panic, a stampede occurred and two people were trampled to death. Cargo was thrown into the sea to try to right the ship. The Joola just barely fared the storm, limping its way into port the next morning in Dakar, listing badly to one side.

When we heard this news, we thanked God for watching over William, and for making it so we were not on that ferry with our 2 and 4-year old! Several years later, in 2002, the ferry did sink in a similar storm, and 1,863 people died. Anyway, God saved us from a very dangerous and traumatic experience for which I was very grateful. Thank You, Lord, for your promise in Psalm 121:7-8 that says:

> *"The Lord will keep you from all harm –*
> *he will watch over your life;*
> *the Lord will watch over your coming and going*
> *both now and forevermore."*

A Whale of a Story

September 24, 1995

STONE:

God protected Kevin's head-first backward fall onto the cement floor in Diembering with his stuffed whale.

When Kevin was two years old, he climbed up on a table in the kid's school room in our house in Diembering. Under his arm he was holding one of his favorite stuffed animals, a big blue whale. Steve told him to get down off the table. Still clinging to his stuffed animal, Kevin lost his balance, teetered backwards, falling head first toward the cement floor.

God's angels were watching over him because somehow in the fall the stuffed animal released from his arm and by the time Kevin hit the floor, the animal was positioned right under his head! Only God could have watched over Kevin in this way, because the stuffed animal was in front of him rather than behind him when he started his fall backwards. God protected my little one from what could have possibly been a very bad head injury!

My Third Child

September 19, 1994 and February 11, 1996

<u>STONE:</u>
God fulfilled a promise to me that the children of Diembering are my 3rd child.

Before Steve and I got married, we discussed the issue of children and how many we'd want to have. Steve was sure that he would only want two. Although I would have preferred three, I was okay with his preference.

When Kevin was a year old, I thought I might be pregnant with a third child. I was secretly very excited about this possibility, because it was what I had always wanted but never dreamed of having. But the pregnancy test came back negative.

As I lay on my bed breastfeeding Kevin and putting him to sleep, I thought about my desire to have a third child. "Why am I not pregnant with a third?" I asked God. Then God 'whispered' to my spirit, "The children of Diembering are your third child. Care for them as you would a third. They are your third child and I give them to you today. Feed my sheep."

With that encouragement and with a new peace in my heart, I started pouring myself into loving the kids in the village.

One day about a year and a half later, I remembered the promise God had made me about the children of Diembering being my third child. On that day I arrived in church to find it FULL of kids – 30 of them! During the worship time they filled the small chapel, along with the 8 other adults. The kids came for Sunday school, which I held right outside the church on mats. There they heard stories about God in their own language. They colored verses in their language and brought them home to fill their dreary mud huts with colorful messages of God's love.

The children of Diembering had become my "third child" and I realized that God was using me to feed His sheep. God's ways are not my ways, but they end up being so much better!

Rice in a Wicker Basket

March 4, 1996

STONE:

God answered my prayer for having closer Kwatay kin after a beach prayer walk. Waay Safietu came bearing rice, asking to be my mom.

> *"I want everything for God, and nothing for me.*
> *I want everything of God, and nothing of me."*

One afternoon, five years into our village time in Senegal, I went for a walk on the beach and poured out my heart to the Lord. I told Him of my frustration over the lack of fruit in my ministry as well as the lack of deep relationships with the people in our village. God then gave me the two thoughts above and sent me back home encouraged – encouraged that it would be Him and not me to do it.

That very same afternoon, Hélène came over to visit and to read Kwatay books with me. Then that evening I was warmly greeted by all the ladies of Halouja who came to our courtyard and had a dance in appreciation of our being there. And the next day a "waay" (older women) came by bringing me rice in a wicker basket and saying that she wanted to be my village mother.

Wow! The Lord couldn't have been more direct in showing me that it was He who would bring about the relationships as well as the fruit if I would just wait and rely on Him.

Who But You?

April 6, 1997

STONE:

God fulfils the promise of Psalm 126:6 at the dedication of the first half of the Kwatay Bible and the Literacy Center.

The culmination of our first six years of work among the Kwatay was seen on April 5th at the Dedication of the first half of the New Testament as well as the opening of the Literacy Center. As one old Kwatay man told us after the celebration, "It was the best party we've had in ten or twenty years!" And it was true. We had everything a big Kwatay party should have:

- enough rice and beef for the whole village, with leftovers
- the "orcastre" of Bukot, who animated the celebration with live music a good part of the day
- the "etakaay" – young men who danced the wrestling dance (a gift to us!)
- music (blaring) when other things were not going on
- a fantastic sit-down meal for the guests of honor
- a well organized literacy competition with fantastic prizes (soccer balls, cloth, books)
- dancing most of the evening (till 11:00 p.m. or so)

The Literacy Center looked absolutely beautiful on the dedication day. The last coat of paint had just been finished the day before. Flowers decorated the fence out front and were placed on the tables. The bookshelves were filled with Kwatay, French and English books – but primarily Kwatay. The aerial photos we had taken of Diembering were hung on the walls of the classroom, and there were beautiful sand signs around the center to identify the different rooms.

All that Wycliffe Bible Translators was meant to be and do was summarized in the celebration that day. It encompassed both Scripture in the mother tongue and literacy, with the whole people group joining together to celebrate these two things. It was the perfect blend that is normally so hard to combine. Not only that, but both Catholics and Protestants worked together to accomplish the feat. What a blessing we'd been given both in our literacy committee and our translation team.

My heart was full of thanks to God. "Lord, who but You could have pulled all this together? Who but You could have given such harmony and unity and purpose among our team here? Who but You could have brought together everything we needed to finish the Literacy Center on time (straw for the roof, paint for the walls, and painters)? Who but You could have blessed a celebration with no arguments, no fighting, and with such festivity? Who but You could have cancelled the meeting scheduled the same day for officials in Ziguinchor, thus allowing Lai Diatta and the Sous Prefet to join us? Who but You could cause such peace and unity among all the people regardless of their religion (Animists, Muslims, Catholics, Protestants), especially with half the speeches focused on the Word of God in their mother tongue? Who but You could have placed a Kwatay evangelist, Ouffi Boly, among us at such a crucial time as this when the people are now ready and open to hear more? Who but You could have worked in the hearts of the young people to come and offer us a surprise gift of their traditional wrestling dance, which is only ever done during the 2-3 week wrestling season each October? Who but You could have kept people from dying during the three days before the Dedication and on our big day? Who but You could pull this together only a week before our departure to Dakar and then on to our furlough time in the USA?"

As Ouffi said in church the following day, "If you think you saw amazing things yesterday, you haven't seen anything yet. God is going to do great things here among us, even greater than what you've just seen. He has so much in store for us." He also said, "What you saw yesterday (the celebration of God's Word in Kwatay) is a sign that we are in the end times.

For God says that when every tongue and people know about Jesus and can hear the Good News in their own mother tongue, the end is near."

God spoke to my heart saying, "Laura, your work and Steve's has not been in vain."

All the struggles, all the tears, all the longings for 'Egypt' (America), all the pain of separation from family during Nika and Kevin's early childhood years, all the frustration learning French and then Kwatay, all the cultural differences that had to be hurdled to be an 'Awaat' (one of them) – we persevered through all these things and many more to get to this point where we could see that our labor had not been in vain. We poured ourselves into the work that God called us to, but it is He who made the work come to fruition and not be in vain. He fulfilled the promise He gave to Steve before we were married, as it says in Psalm 126:5-6:

> *"Those who sow with tears*
> *will reap with songs of joy.*
> *Those who go out weeping,*
> *carrying seed to sow,*
> *will return with songs of joy,*
> *carrying sheaves with them."*

White Leather Sandals

June 15, 1997

STONE:

God provided the exact white leather sandals I couldn't afford, brand new, at a thrift store, two furloughs in a row!

On our first furlough in 1993, I wanted to get a certain pair of sandals – leather shoes with white straps made by Bass. Well, because they cost quite a bit and Steve doesn't like spending money unnecessarily, I didn't get them that summer when we were in Maine, which is the time they were available and "in season".

One day that fall I ended up going to a children's thrift shop in Beverly, Massachusetts, looking for clothes for Nika and Kevin. What I saw in the corner along with all the other shoes made my mouth drop open: the EXACT style, color and size sandal I wanted! The lady at the register said they were dropped off the day before and she hadn't even had a chance to mark a price on them. She gave them to me for a dollar! Not only that, but they were BRAND NEW! Well, I couldn't help but rejoice at the thought of how God was looking down from Heaven and rejoicing with me. He placed those shoes there for me, making His love and care for me so personal and giving me such great inner joy.

When I returned home on furlough four years later, I again needed new sandals. What I really wanted were the exact same shoes that God had miraculously supplied for me four years before. I looked at a pair at a Bass Outlet in Gilroy, California, but they were so expensive ($25). I though Steve might not be happy if I purchased them. Money was tight and he always got cheaper shoes at discount stores.

A month later I was in a thrift shop in Mount Shasta and I noticed among the shoes there the exact pair of sandals I wanted: the EXACT style, color and size. Not only that, but once again they were BRAND NEW, just like four years earlier! I laughed out loud, rejoicing in God's amazing goodness, and His love and care for me. I feel like He honored me with the desire of my heart for my having honored the wishes of my husband. God truly is amazing in His blessings to those who wait for Him.

Greater Than a Waiting List

August 17, 1997

STONE:

God opened up a spot for Nika at Covenant Christian School when the class was full and there was a waiting list.

On our second furlough, in 1997, Nika was going to be entering first grade. We thought it would be a great experience for her to go to a Christian school for the half year we'd be on the North Shore in Massachusetts. We wrote to friends there asking them to send us information about Christian schools in the area but they didn't follow through.

Finally in mid-July we got information on two Christian schools, but unfortunately by that time they were both full and had waiting lists. I still sent in the application forms, praying that God would graciously open a door for Nika to go to a Christian school, and in particular Covenant Christian, which was located close to us in Beverly.

When Tom Stoner, the principal at Covenant Christian, read our application, he felt moved by God to make an unusual exception and ask the board of directors to accept Nika for the fall session. Even though there was a waiting list, they bumped Nika ahead of the others and even made the class size larger than normal to accommodate her. God heard our prayers and answered. He gave Nika an amazing teacher and wonderful classmates and she grew in her love for God there.

At the same time we were trying to get Nika into a Christian primary school, we were also calling Christian pre-schools in the area so that Kevin could attend a few mornings a week. One day after spending two hours on the phone, I learned of a school only a short walk from where we were staying, and they had one spot left for the fall session. It has been so amazing to see God's hand in caring for and blessing our kids.

Radiating Light

January 11 and 24, 1998

STONE:

God-light radiating from Steve and me at NewLife church service during our furlough.

A t the end of our second furlough, in January of 1998, Steve and I went to our last speaking engagement which was at a church that we had never been to before: NewLife Christian Fellowship in Connecticut. They wanted to know more about missions and to hear about our work in Senegal.

After the service was over, a lady came up to us with tears in her eyes saying she had to tell us something. She said that when Steve was up front talking with the kids and I was sitting opposite him, there was a light that shone all around his head and body. Then when the pastor got up, there was light around him too. She realized that the light was radiating from me as I sat in the front row just before him. We drank in what she shared, and as soon as she finished speaking, it seemed like she just disappeared from sight. We looked around for her later but never saw her again.

As I look back on it, I feel like God was trying to show us that He was with us. We were about to embark on our final term to finish the New Testament in Kwatay – a term which turned out to be the most difficult time we were to have in Senegal. Many times in the months ahead I remembered back to that day's unusual happening and took courage to press on when everything in me wanted to quit. God knows when we need special encouragement, and that truly was one of those times.

Heart-Shaped Cloud

February 22, 1998

STONE:

Enjoying God's presence on the SIL rooftop and God smiling back through a heart-shaped cloud.

In 1998 we returned to Dakar, but soon found out we couldn't return to the village due to continued rebel activity and unrest in the Casamance. We ended up staying in an apartment on the SIL center which made privacy and solitude difficult. So I resorted to going up on the roof of the SIL building in order to have quiet times with the Lord.

One night after dinner I went up on the roof to pray. That night my prayer time was extra special. It was so nice just talking to God and waiting for Him to talk back to me through His Spirit. After talking to Him a while, I realized just how much I enjoyed being up there on the roof and talking with Him. It was more special than having time alone with my good friend, Marcia – and I told Him so. Saying that from the heart felt so good because I had always hoped that it would be so. I always wanted Jesus to be my best friend, even though I still needed other people to talk to when something was heavy on my heart.

I walked around the roof a few more minutes, enjoying His presence. Then when I looked up in the sky I saw a bright light coming through the clouds which were in the shape of a heart and had a smile in the middle. No joke!!! I laughed to myself and thought how God must be feeling at that moment: much loved and very pleased. This made my joy complete.

Something Green Moving

January 10, 1999

God protected Kevin from a poisonous viper in a hole in our porch in Diembering.

One day towards the end of our New Testament translation project in Diembering, we were having a lunch for literacy workers in our gazebo. When the meal was finished, all the adults sat on the circle of wooden benches to talk while the kids went over to the house to play. I looked over every once in a while to keep my eyes on our two children.

At one point, I saw Kevin, who was five years old, bending down on the porch and poking his finger into one of the many holes in the old concrete. I decided to walk over and see what he was up to. As I walked over, Nika came up to me and said that Kevin had seen something green moving in the hole and thought maybe there was a frog there, so he was trying to get it out. I immediately told him to get his finger out of the hole, and then went to ask the guys in the gazebo to come check it out. They looked in the hole and said there was a poisonous viper there!

They told me to boil some water and after pouring it down the hole, a long snake came slithering out, which the waiting crowd promptly beat with sticks. Once again, God protected my little boy from harm.

Thrown Away Dreams

October 19, 1999

STONE:

After throwing out pictures of our future "dream house", God healed my arm.

After ten years of moving from the village to Dakar and back every few months, I was desiring so much to settle down and have a place of our own. Over the years I'd collected photos from Better Homes and Gardens and other magazines of what I'd want my future dream home to look like. I had them all in a folder ready for the day that we could be "normal" and own our own home.

Upon completion of the New Testament, we had to make yet another move, this time to Dallas to typeset the New Testament. I did a lot of heavy lifting during that move and pulled a muscle in my arm. I couldn't lift my arm without significant pain, and there was no way I could play tennis, which I really missed.

One evening I was praying and felt that God wanted me to get rid of all the photos I had collected of houses from various magazines – my dreams of what I wanted my future home to look like. With a very heavy heart, but in obedience to the Lord, I put them all in the trash – my hopes of a future home now completely gone. Immediately after being obedient and giving these hopes and dreams over to God, I had no more ache and pain in my arm AT ALL. I truly couldn't believe it!!!

There were three times when God had specifically said to me, "Do not pursue having a home." (5/1/1999, 9/5/1999, and this time). His point was clear – now wasn't the time to settle down in the States. He had something better in store for me, and He confirmed that when He blessed me by instantly healing my arm. His hopes and dreams for me always turn out infinitely more fulfilling than my own!

The Other Side of the World

October 19 - December 9, 1999

God leading us to Vanuatu by shutting the door to having a home now in the USA and making a perfect fit and confirming our going to the South Pacific.

As Steve and I were finishing the Kwatay New Testament in 1999, we started considering our next steps. We knew we couldn't stay in Senegal as Steve withered in the big city, and we couldn't remain in the village due to continued rebel activity in the Casamance region. We considered other places in Africa but realized that anywhere we went we'd have to be located in big cities and we knew that wouldn't work. The only other French-speaking allocation would be in Vanuatu and New Caledonia in the South Pacific.

When we were typesetting the New Testament in Dallas, we set up a meeting to discuss these possibilities with Neville Southwell, the SIL Pacific Area Director. The morning of our meeting, God led me to read Nehemiah 1-2. Then during our meeting, in the same way that God gave favor from the king to Nehemiah to carry out work in a distant place, God also granted us favor in Neville's sight to work in the Pacific. In the same way Nehemiah asked for letters to the governors for his work, we also needed a letter of invitation to work there. And in the same way Nehemiah wanted to rebuild and help those in disgrace, we wanted to help out the SIL branches that were needing to rebuild after several situations involving moral disgrace and disunity.

Wanting more confirmation from the Lord, I asked God for a sign by having someone or something talk about Vanuatu that week (as I'd done for Senegal ten years earlier). That Wednesday I went to my Bible study in Dallas and a new lady came who couldn't stop talking about Vanuatu. She and her family had been there and were hoping to go back. This totally surprised me as when we had asked Neville if there was anyone else in Dallas who we could talk to about Vanuatu for more information, he said there was no one else who had been there.

Another confirmation came that week as well. One morning when I woke up I read Psalm 143, and my eyes kept going back to verse 8:

> *"Let the morning bring me word*
> *of your unfailing love,*
> *for I have put my trust in you.*
> *Show me the way I should go,*
> *for to you I entrust my life."*

I knew God would somehow confirm the direction of our path that morning. Immediately after this, Steve came in and the first thing out of his mouth was, "You won't believe the email we just got from Margaret Hill." I said, "Oh no, it's going to be bad. She's going to want us to stay in Senegal and do consulting there." But here were her words to us:

> "You may be surprised at this, but even though
> I'm sorry for the Senegal Branch not to be
> getting you back long term, I actually had a
> sense of rightness about what you are doing
> when I read your message. Where exactly will
> you be going? A little island in the middle of the
> ocean?"

The final confirmation came on our last Sunday in Dallas, attending Hill Crest Baptist Church. The pastor had been going through the book of Corinthians, but said that he felt led to change his message that week to the first few chapters of Nehemiah – stressing the need to complete what God has called one to do. My heart was so encouraged by this as those were the exact same chapters God had me read before our meeting with Neville to talk about the possibility of working in the South Pacific.

God seemed to clearly be leading us to a new corner of the world, and we were excited to see what He had planned!

Bibles in Baskets

May 21-25, 2000

STONE:

God completes the promise of Psalm 126:5-6 with the dedication of the Kwatay New Testament, the JESUS Film, and changed hearts.

As Steve and I were first preparing to go out with Wycliffe to do a translation project, God encouraged us with the verse in Psalm 126:5 which says,

"Those who sow with tears will reap with songs of joy."

There had been many tears and hardships during the 10 years we had translated the New Testament into Kwatay, but now we stood at the moment where God had said that "songs of joy" would come. The Kwatay New Testament had been typeset in Dallas, printed in Korea, and now the dedication in Diembering was set for May of 2000.

In a village where the majority of the Kwatay people were animists, we were not sure how people would react to this special day. We had planned a feast for the whole village, and everyone came out to celebrate, dance, and participate in the festivities. When the women came into the main town square, carrying Bibles in baskets on their heads, they celebrated by giving each other high fives. They wore their traditional blue pagnes and white t-shirts. Many people commented about the speeches and how they were touched by them. Ouffi later told us that now people would no longer mock the fledgling evangelical church but would hold it in higher esteem.

That night we had the premier showing of the JESUS Film in the small church. The place was jammed, and some people even tried hanging from the windows outside in order to get a glimpse of the film. People listened intently as they watched the first-ever film in their language. How incredible to see God's Word come alive for the Kwatay people!!!

The next day our little church was filled for the Sunday service. We had lots of good singing (unfortunately I had laryngitis), testimonies (around 7 people shared), and a sermon by Ouffi. At the end of the message, Ouffi said something that hit both Steve and I. He said that we should not worry about leaving them, but that he would write and we would have tears of joy hearing of God's ongoing work among the Kwatay people. Again, it reminded us of the verse God gave both of us in Psalm 126:5,

"Those who sow with tears will reap with songs of joy."

God was faithful to keep us through tough times in order to accomplish His purposes for the Kwatay people.

Please, Not the Sack

June 4 and August 22, 2000

STONE:

God protected us when rebels attacked our truck after the New Testament dedication. Len's dream and prayers heard.

A week after the dedication of the Kwatay New Testament, we prepared for our departure back to Dakar. It was a very emotional time for everyone as it would be our last day among the Kwatay. I went for a prayer walk around the village and couldn't hold back the tears.

Later that morning we met with the believers to pray one last time in our living room before driving to Ziguinchor to catch the Joola ferry for Dakar. The believers told us how much we'd meant to them and all we'd done for them. Jean Paul, who was next to me, bowed his head and I saw tears falling to the ground, making big wet splotches on the cement floor in our living room. Steve encouraged the believers to stand firm in love and unity and said we'd be praying for them. We then prayed, and that's when I really lost it. I just couldn't hold back the tears – these people meant so much to me.

Pastor Ouffi had us all stand and hold hands for the last prayer. He prayed that just as Moses asked God to go Himself with the children of Israel, and not just send His angel, that God Himself would accompany us on our trip out to Ziguinchor and onward.

Steve and I went around the circle of believers shaking their hands and when I got to Ouffi, I shook his hand but he proceeded to give me an American-style hug. That really touched me, as that is exactly what I wanted to do with each believer there. We then got in the pickup we'd borrowed from the Manning's and drove off down the road toward Cap Skirring, rejoicing in all that God had done the last few weeks and years.

We were totally at peace as we navigated the truck down the lone track through the jungle. We talked about the joy and fulfillment we had experienced working among the Kwatay, as hard as it had been at times. We talked about the ministry Steve had on his heart to take pictures and video for teams in Vanuatu, and how happy we were with the equipment we had. We talked about how abnormally at ease we were driving on the road out to Ziguinchor – the road most known for rebel attacks in the past. We felt that after the prayers of the saints in Diembering, nothing could happen!

Then a man stepped out into the road and waved us down. People were always wanting us to stop and pick them up – this seemed like just another, but this time we didn't have any extra room for additional passengers. Then I saw the gun he was hiding behind his body, but Steve didn't. He kept driving, meaning to pass by, and I was tongue tied – literally I couldn't speak! Right as we drove past, the man swung up the gun and a staccato round of ten shots slammed into the truck.

Knowing we couldn't outrun more bullets, Steve hit the brakes. We could smell gas (thankfully the truck we had borrowed was a diesel) and a bullet had shattered the front windshield by Steve's head. God went with us. He was there guiding our steps, protecting us.

The man with the automatic assault rifle ran up to my window and demanded money. He was both nervous and high strung, probably on drugs, as his eyes were wild and the whites were showing. I reached into our backpack in the front seat and pulled out the money which Steve had placed in a sock. It also had a camera flash in it. The rebel didn't see the money at the bottom of the sock but only felt the camera flash. He came back to the window and again demanded money. As I looked in the backpack for our second stash he saw the camera equipment, grabbed the whole backpack and wrenched it through the window. "Oh no, not the sack," Steve gasped. Not only did it have all our camera and video equipment, but also all the film and video footage we had taken the last month of the dedication, the baptism and our friends in the village. It had our passports and health certificates. It had Steve's prescription glasses and work papers. It also had $2,000 in CFA from extra money we'd had for the dedication celebration and the sale of our refrigerator and other household items. Our hearts sunk.

The man still couldn't find any money in the backpack and this time as he came back to the window he was really mad. Steve asked if he could get out of the truck to show him where the money was. With his hands raised he opened the door and got out. He got the sock and showed the rebel the money inside. He also showed him the money that was hidden in the sack.

Distressed to have lost all the photos of our last month in the village, Steve asked if he could take out the roll of film in the camera (forgetting, in the pressure of the moment, all the other rolls of exposed film in the backpack). The rebel said okay, but to do it quickly. Steve then dared to asked for the other things in the sack that were not important to the rebels – our passports, important papers, etc. The rebel motioned Steve over to the woods at the side of the road, but it was then that Steve got a bit scared. There was another rebel there who was now holding the backpack, and he removed a gleaming knife as Steve approached. Steve decided it was time to forget about our possessions and to start concentrating on just being allowed to leave.

But just at that moment, another car drove up. The rebel's focus was now drawn away from Steve as he brandished his weapon and stopped the other unfortunate car. In it were four people. Once again the rebel demanded money. The woman in the back seat got out some, but as he went to the back window to take it from her he saw that the person in the front seat was a soldier with a rifle (pointed the other way). He tried to grab the man's rifle, but when he didn't let it go, the rebel stepped back and shot him, spraying the car with bullets.

Steve had been out behind our truck while all this was happening, and the truck was piled high with the things from our move so that the kids and I couldn't see out the back. We didn't even know another car had come on the scene. When we heard the shots, we feared they had just shot Steve. But when the rebel started shooting, Steve ran back to our truck to take cover. We were so relieved he was still alive and urged him to quickly get in so we could leave. But Steve looked back and saw the rebels scurrying into the woods, and he wanted to go back to the other car to see if he could help the people there.

When he arrived, one man was twitching in death, another was dead and the driver was wounded. The woman was alive, but Steve didn't know it at the time because it was dark in the back seat and the woman was silent and didn't move, fearing it was the rebel who had come back. Steve returned to our vehicle and I pleaded with him to get us out of there. We drove several miles to the next military outpost and told them what had happened. They sent troops back to help the other car and to look for the rebels. Soon we heard the sound of heavy artillery as they ineffectually fired rounds into the surrounding jungle.

We waited at Niassia for two hours while they searched the area for the rebels. When we finally reached our destination at the WEC compound in Ziguinchor, peace finally came over me. Release. No more threat. No more danger. Breathe. We called the folks at SIL in Dakar to let them know what had happened. Then we took the kids to a pool at a hotel to decompress and debrief.

There was much to be thankful for. God didn't allow the kids or me to see any of the killing. We just crouched low in the cabin of the pickup and prayed for Steve's safety. Secondly, the rebels had not been unnecessarily malicious toward us – even though they shot at our truck, it was to stop us. Miraculously we were all okay. One bullet passed within inches of my head before shattering the windshield right in front of Steve, and one bullet went through the kid's door and through the seat inches below them, before piercing the gas tank. The rebels took only the one backpack and nothing else, for which we were thankful (they had just started asking Steve what was in the back of the truck when the other car arrived on the scene). We were thankful that we had not been pulled off the road into the bush and never heard from again, which had happened periodically to other people.

Before I went to bed that evening, I read the following passage in Psalm 73:25-28,

> *"Whom have I in heaven but You?*
> *And earth has nothing I desire besides you.*
> *My flesh and my heart may fail,*
> *but God is the strength of my heart*
> *and my portion forever.*
> *Those who are far from you will perish;*
> *you destroy all who are unfaithful to you.*
> *But as for me, it is good to be near God.*
> *I have made the Sovereign Lord my refuge;*
> *I will tell of all your deeds."*

Truly God was our refuge! He is the strength of my heart and my portion forever. Praise the Lord!

Two months later we received an email from Len Giatas. He said that a few years ago, after our second furlough, he had a dream that rebels were shooting at us with automatic weapons. Since then, whenever he prayed for us, he would pray God's protection over us. He never told us about the dream because he didn't want to scare us. He was even wondering why God gave it to him, because he knew we were now leaving the village and what he'd seen in his dream had never happened. Then he received our June 2000 Peeks newsletter describing the shooting and he finally understood why God had given him that revelation and why God had laid it so heavy on his heart to pray for us all that time.

Thank You, Lord, because You knew all the details of that eventful day years in advance and You were already planning our deliverance. Thank You for revealing this in advance to our friend, because it shows me even more fully how You are in control and can be trusted.

Petting Dolphins

August 22, 2000

STONE:

Nika praying for a chance to pet a dolphin at Marine World months in advance. And she was chosen!

Sandwiched between finishing up our work in Senegal and moving on to our new work in Vanuatu, we visited the grandparents in California. Months before, while we were still in Senegal, Nika knew that we would be going to Marine World, and she started praying that she'd be able to pet a dolphin there (she was nine years old and totally into dolphins at the time, as we would see them occasionally when taking the ferry to Dakar).

When we arrived at Marine World, we asked the workers there if Nika could be a volunteer for the dolphin show, but they said they only choose one person from the crowd of thousands and that it was random – totally up to the person conducting the show. So we got to the show 45 minutes early, hoping to get front row seats so that Nika could be chosen to help in the show. Nika mentioned to one of the girls working at Marine World how she'd love to help. And we could see others asking as well.

Ten minutes before the show started, one of the helpers came up and asked Nika if she wanted to come up on stage as a volunteer to help in the show and pet the dolphins. What a NEAT gift from God! God touched everyone's heart by answering Nika's prayers. Even Grandma Kay was moved by it, and that evening wanted to show all the relatives the video Steve took of it.

God is such an amazingly personal God, who delights to respond to the prayers of His children!

Accepting My Lot

October 16, 2000

STONE:

My wrist was immediately healed on Epi, giving me confirmation from the Lord of being in Vanuatu.

After arriving in Vanuatu and spending some time on the island of Epi, Steve and I starting questioning the viability of language projects in the island nation because of the high level of bilingualism in Bislama. I'd also been struggling with the fact that there were so many Christians there. Were we really needed there when in other parts of the world people were perishing without knowing God?

I told Steve that I had to have a purpose in Vanuatu and I had to know that it was important to the missionary effort. As I said this, Steve was rubbing my sore wrist and it was hurting so much I told him to stop. I'd had a sore wrist since arriving in Vanuatu, and it had gotten worse since coming out to Epi for our village stay. Steve was surprised at how much it hurt. I told him it reminded me of him having wrist issues as he struggled with accepting having to live in the city for a time when we were in Senegal, and then how God had made his wrist noticeably better since leaving there.

Anyway, as I thought of Steve's difficulty in accepting his lot in Senegal (although he had to stick it out), so right now I was having difficulty accepting my lot being in Vanuatu. I decided in my heart that if this was true, and that if God wanted me to stop questioning His leading and accept being there, that I would move my wrist, and if it was better and didn't hurt, then that would be God showing me He wanted us there in Vanuatu. I gingerly moved my wrist and found that it didn't hurt AT ALL. It was completely better!

God instantly healed my wrist to convince me that He had brought us to Vanuatu for a reason and not to question His leading. God knew that I'd need this encouragement and confirmation for the rocky road ahead.

Luke Partnership Projects

July 6, 2002

STONE:

Awoke that day knowing God would lead us in our future work. Katy Barnwell wrote concerning doing a Luke Partnership.

During our two years serving in Vanuatu, Steve was continually getting resistance from the translation teams to follow translation principles that were necessary for producing quality translations. With no support from the director, we decided to keep our eyes open for what God might have for us next. We didn't see any possibilities for staying in Wycliffe and doing Bible translation work, so we were thinking of returning to the States to work in editorial work or business management.

One morning, I woke up with God impressing on me that this was the day He was going to lead us into our future work. Steve came into our bedroom a few minutes later and said that Katy Barnwell had just written concerning our helping out with Luke Partnership projects in French-speaking Africa. We had never considered this, but it seemed perfect for us as we could base ourselves in the States and Steve could travel overseas to run workshops and do consultant checks. It seemed so "right" and God gave me the heads-up in advance to know it was from Him. I just love how God leads us and confirms our next steps!

73

Cyclones and Prayers

December 28, 2002

STONE:

Class 5 Cyclone Zoe turned 150° away from Vanuatu right as it approached.

A few months before our departure from Vanuatu, I had a gut feeling like I was going to die. A week later, a class 5 hurricane called Zoe was heading straight for the Island of Efate where we were located just outside of Port Vila. The hurricane was predicted to hit our island with sustained winds of 150 mph with gusts over 200 mph, and a storm surge of 39 feet. This was the largest-ever recorded cyclone in the South Pacific. And there was no place we could go to escape its path.

We immediately sent out a Petite Peeks email to implore our supporters to pray for us and that Island nation. As the outer winds of the hurricane started to blow, we boarded up our windows. Then just hours before the storm's arrival, there was a sudden change in direction of the hurricane. It made a 150 degree turn away from Efate and headed back out to sea.

No one could explain how the hurricane changed course this drastically when it was so close to hitting the shores of Vanuatu. We know that God answered the cries of His people and had mercy not only on us but on the people of Vanuatu. The "gut feeling" I had that I was going to die was a warning of this imminent, unforeseen danger. God decided He had more work for us yet to do, for which I am truly grateful!

Camera Batteries

January 5, 2003

STONE:

Prayed for Nika's camera to work and God made it work!

When we lived in Vanuatu, we'd often go to a pool at a resort on our day off. When we returned home from the pool one Saturday, Nika's camera wouldn't work. Steve spent a half hour trying to fix it but couldn't. When I got out of the shower, I felt God telling me to go and pray with Nika about her camera. So I went in and closed the door and we prayed together concerning it, asking God to help it work, or for wisdom to know how we might possibly get it to work again.

After praying, I asked Nika if I could see the camera and asked what wasn't working. I then switched the batteries around and it worked. Steve later told us he had done this MANY times already and it hadn't worked, but God let it work this time to show us that yes, He is personal. Yes, He does care. Yes, He does want us to come to Him with our concerns. Nika and I praised God for this answer to prayer.

That 0.01% Chance

January 28, 2004 and February 8, 2004

<u>STONE:</u>
God leading us to our home in Grants Pass and how it matched up with our requests to God.

On our return to the States, our whole family had hopes and dreams to find not just a house in Southern Oregon, but to find our dream home. Steve and I even wrote down a list of what we prayed our new place would be like:

- quiet
- rural
- mountains
- view of lake or river
- larger lot – not on top of other houses
- not too cold
- town within 15 minute drive
- big store within one hour drive
- airport within 3 hour drive
- good school system
- Christian school
- tennis courts

Unfortunately most of the houses we looked at in our price range were either "dives" or we were divided in our opinions on them. Nothing seemed right and all fell far short of our dream house.

One morning we all piled into our realtor's van and headed for what seemed like a perfect place out on Highway 238 in the Applegate area. Unfortunately the house was dark, dingy, and close to a noisy highway. As we were driving back through North Applegate, I looked out to the hillside on the right and said, "Isn't this area just beautiful? That would be a nice place to live." We headed around on 238 and came to North

Applegate road and as Phil (our realtor) passed it he said, "Do you want me to drive up that way to look at the area?" I said, "Yes, let's turn back."

So we turned around and started driving down the road. It was a gorgeous country area with nice homes set back from the street. Phil then saw a real estate sign at the base of a road we were passing and said, "Do you want to go up and take a look?" I said, "Sure!" At this point Steve told him, "What's the chance of finding a house like this, like 0.01%? I mean, we've already seen everything in our price range on the MLS." Phil answered, "You'd be surprised – it happens more often than you'd expect."

We spotted a sign on the left while heading up Board Shanty but it wasn't the Prudential sign we had seen at the base of the hill. Phil said, "Do you want to look?" Of course the kids and I were all for it ☺! He pulled up to the sign but there weren't any flyers in the box describing the house. I urged him to drive down the driveway so we can see the place. We curved down and a blue split-level house appeared that seemed just right. All four of us were "wowing".

Phil called the real estate company on the flyer to get the code for the lockbox. We went in and looked around and immediately knew it was the perfect place for us. Nika saw horses next door, the mountain views were amazing, it was peaceful and had a seasonal pond and stream, there was a yard for Kevin to play soccer in, the open floor plan was light and spacious, and the list went on! Everything about it just said "home" to me. Only two things weren't right. The price and no office for Steve, since he was going to be working out of the house.

Thankfully the house had been on the market for several months and the owner was eager to sell. After meeting with us he agreed to reduce the price substantially, exactly to the high point we had been prepared to pay (and this was in a market where houses were selling at the asking price). As for an office, Steve decided he could put a desk in our bedroom and make it a combined bedroom/office.

So God gave us a very special gift and we knew that it was directly from Him. When we had no hope left of finding a decent house, much less our dream home, God provided what we had hoped for and so much more! And He did it in such a way that we could unequivocally say, "That was a God thing!"

A Home of Their Own

May 21, 2004

STONE:

God confirmed that our Grants Pass home was where He wanted us – a gift from Him.

A few months after moving into our home in Grants Pass, I started to feel guilty about being in such a nice place and loving it so much. It seemed too good to be true, a comfortable life in stark contrast to the life we had previously lived overseas as "real missionaries". Was this new home REALLY from the Lord, I wondered, or did we miss His perfect will and plan for our lives by settling down here?

So one morning during my quiet time I poured out my heart to the Lord. Condemnation was plaguing me, so I asked Him to speak to my heart on this issue. Did He want us to be in our Grants Pass home or not? As I asked Him, I remember thinking, "How would He ever make His will on this known to me so that I could finally be 'at peace'?".

But I opened His Word anyway and started reading in 1 Chronicles 17, continuing where I'd left off the previous day as I read through the Bible in one year. I got to verse 9 and stopped in my tracks. It said,

> *"And I will provide a place for my people Israel and will plant them so that they can have a home of their own and no longer be disturbed."*

Then in verse 10 God says,

> *"The Lord will build a house for you."*

God put my heart to rest that morning as He confirmed that we were in His will and that this house was His gift to us – a place of peace and rest that we could enjoy. I just love how God talks to us through His Word, and responds directly to our situations.

Heavy Hearts and Dreams

September 1, 2004

<u>STONE:</u>

God answered my question to know if Eric would be okay after brain surgery, gifting me with peace.

For my parents' 50th wedding anniversary, they took the whole Schluntz family on a cruise in Alaska to celebrate. Two weeks after we arrived home I got an unusual call from my mom. She said she had just talked with my brother Eric on the phone and he seemed quite sick with the flu and didn't even know what day it was. I told her that was not usual for the flu and they needed to drive down to Marlborough to check up on him.

The next day my dad went over to make sure he was okay. When he arrived, he found Eric incoherent and the house a wreck. He immediately loaded Eric in the car and drove to the urgent care center in Marlborough. After a scan, they located a large brain tumor and quickly medevaced him by helicopter to a larger hospital in Hartford. After more tests, the doctors scheduled surgery for the next morning.

All day long I was grieving at the possibility of losing Eric. He was only 45 and we had always been so close – how could this be happening? I wanted to fly out immediately to be there, but Mom said to wait until after the surgery to see how he would do. I prayed and fasted until dinner. Still heavy in heart, I cried myself to sleep. In the middle of the night I woke up and couldn't get back to sleep. So I asked God to give me a heart of peace and to give me some word of what would happen to Eric in my dreams.

I ended up dozing off and awoke the next morning remembering two dreams in which Eric was just fine after the surgery. Finally my troubled heart had total peace. No longer did I worry about losing Eric, but praised God that He would bring my brother through okay. What a contrast to how I had felt the day before as I was grieving!

Later that morning, I got news from my folks that the surgery was successful and that they had been able to get most of the tumor out of his right lobe. Eric still had a long road to recovery, but he would live and remain a part of our lives for some time.

God meets us in our distress, calming our fears and answering our prayers as we turn to Him.

Two Men in Black

October 31, 2004

STONE:

God saving me from two attackers while I was running on Halloween.

I t was Halloween morning – a Sunday morning – and I decided to go out for an early morning run before the kids woke up. Steve was on his way home from Africa, so as I went out I locked the front door and tied the house key in the laces of my running shoe. We had lived in our home in Grants Pass now for nine months and I was used to going for early morning runs a few times a week. My run consisted of going down Board Shanty Road and North Applegate, then retracing my route back home.

This Halloween morning, as I was slowly jogging back up the steep portion of Board Shanty Road, I noticed an old truck pulled off to the side. It had an open back with a tarp over a bunch of lumpy objects that looked like bodies. It made me shudder and I was glad not to see any people around the vehicle. I continued to jog up the hill when all of a sudden a big guy dressed all in black jumped out of the roadside ditch. He made his way to the center line of the road and started walked directly toward me. I slowed, trying to make up my mind whether to continue or not, when another guy dressed exactly like the first jumped out of the same ditch and joined the man in the middle of the road.

The black clad figures walked side by side down the center of the road directly toward me. They weren't hunters because they weren't carrying guns. But I knew that if they meant to harm me, there would be no way to get past them. And this seemed like the perfect spot for a trap, because there were no houses visible along this part of the road, and they could take me away without anyone seeing or hearing.

With no time to lose, I made a 180° turn and sprinted down the road as fast as I could go, veering into the long driveway winding to the Wassink's house. I knew they had a big black dog but that didn't faze me. I ran right up to their door and pounded urgently. It was only 7:30 a.m. and they answered the door in their pajamas. They were surprised but let me in and I quickly told them my story. After a half hour, Mr. Wassink drove me back up Board Shanty. The old truck and the two guys dressed in black were gone.

This was by far the scariest event I had ever faced in my life. Had the men been apart with one hiding behind the truck and the other ahead of me up the road, I would not have been able to escape. I also couldn't help wondering about my kids who were asleep in the house. Had I not come home, they would have had no idea where I had disappeared to. Worse still was that the key to the house was in my shoe and the guys could have harmed them as well. But God watched over my life that day. He provided a way of escape and turned back my enemy. It was as if the Lord was fulfilling in my life the verses in Zephaniah 3:14-17, which I had read in my quiet time right before I went for my run:

> *"Sing, Daughter Zion;*
> *shout aloud, Israel!*
> *Be glad and rejoice with all your heart,*
> *Daughter Jerusalem!*
> *The Lord had taken away your punishment,*
> *he has turned back your enemy.*
> *The Lord, the King of Israel, is with you;*
> *never again will you fear any harm.*
> *On that day they will say to Jerusalem,*
> *'Do not fear, Zion;*
> *do not let your hands hang limp.*
> *The Lord our God is with you,*
> *the Mighty Warrior who saves.*
> *He will take great delight in you;*
> *in his love he will no longer rebuke you,*
> *but will rejoice over you with singing.'"*

Red Lights and Speeding Cars

October 11, 2005

STONE:

God protected Kevin and me from a bad car accident on 7th and A Street in Grants Pass.

Kryptonite soccer practice had just finished at Grants Pass High School and Kevin and I turned onto A Street and then stopped at the traffic light at 7th Street. The light turned green and the car ahead of us passed through the intersection as normal. I was behind him but noticed something out of the corner of my eye. A vehicle to my left was speeding toward us, even though his traffic light was red. I hit the brakes as he barreled through the red light, narrowly missing us. Kevin and I were both seated on the left hand side of the car, so one or both of us could easily have been injured or killed if I had just followed the first car through the intersection.

I felt like God sent His angels to watch over and protect us, just as it says in Hebrews 1:14,

> *"Are not all angels ministering spirits sent to serve those who will inherit salvation?"*

One Activity Too Many

November 7, 2005

STONE:

God answered my need to have more time by stopping my Sunday School ministry that same day.

After returning to the States and settling in Oregon, I found myself over-committed in my service activities. As I drove to church one Sunday, I told Nika and Marcia (a friend who was visiting) that if I could, I would love to be able to bow out of teaching Sunday School as it not only took a lot of time to prepare, but it was difficult to be there every week with Kevin's soccer schedule. I was already leading two women's Bible studies, preparing for homegroup at my house, doing visitation ministry, and serving on the missions committee. If I had to let something go, the one activity I would choose to stop would be teaching Sunday School.

I arrived at the High School's Performing Arts Center (PAC) that morning – an outreach of River Valley Community Church targeting those who might never want to step foot into a church building – and the children's coordinator came up and told me, "Did you hear? We aren't going to be meeting at the PAC after this Sunday. This is it. No more doubling up on locations. Thanks so much for your help for the time we've been meeting here."

So cool how God hears our deepest concerns even before we bring them to Him!

A Run-Away Horse

February 23, 2006

STONE:

God prompted me to have my quiet time outside before lunch which saved Jasmine from possible injury or loss.

While I was putting clean sheets on the beds one morning, I felt compelled that before lunch I should have a quiet time with the Lord. I also felt like I should go sit on the front porch, which was not my usual place, but I followed the inner leading.

Earlier that morning, I had been gardening and I had left the horse Nika had been given, Jasmine, in her paddock. About ten minutes into my quiet time, Jasmine came along the path, outside her penned area, and started cantering toward our meadow. Wow, did that get my attention! I grabbed some grain and lured her back into the corral and locked the gate. I realized later that I must have left the gate open between our fence and Shelley's, and Jasmine had found a way out.

Anyway, had I not obeyed God's prompting to have a quiet time, and to have it in the location He was leading me to, Jasmine could have taken off down the road without anyone knowing her whereabouts. Thank You, Lord, for blessing me with Your guiding Spirit!

Death of a Dream

January 20 and February 9, 2009

STONE:

God made it clear for me to coach the Hidden Valley High School boys' tennis team.

Death of a dream – that's what it felt like the day I was filling out paperwork to apply for the coaching position for the boy's tennis team at Hidden Valley High School. That same morning I got a call from Kevin who said he broke his right arm snow boarding up on Mount Ashland. I had really wanted to coach the team because Kevin was going to be on it – so what should I do now?

Praying about it, I decided to go ahead and hand in my application, but to only accept the position if NO ONE else would do it. If the team would be in jeopardy of not having a season that year because of not having a coach, then I'd do it. This would be how I would know if I was supposed to serve in this way, with or without Kevin on the team.

Three weeks later, Michael Schaeffer, the athletic director at Hidden Valley, called and asked to meet with me. He said that if I weren't able to be the coach, they were thinking of disbanding the tennis program since there would be no one to head it up. God answered my "fleece" and made His will clear. I then asked Michael what to do about Kevin, since he would be unable to play the first few weeks due to his broken arm. He said that as long as Kevin could make one of the top 12 spots once he was healthy, then to put him on the team.

As it turned out, Kevin started out playing left handed and was better than half the team, so there was no problem giving him one of the spots on the roster! And when he was finally able to switch from his left hand to his right hand, he took over the number one spot.

Entrusting my dreams and hopes to the Lord, He gave me back the desires of my heart.

Seeing Eric Again

September 8, 2010

<u>STONE:</u>

God warned me through a dream in which I saw Eric, of some future pain and to trust God. I was diagnosed five months later with melanoma.

In September of 2010, I had an amazing dream in which I saw my brother Eric for the first time since his death a few years earlier. He looked absolutely perfect – not young or old, but clear, detailed and beautiful. What stood out to me were his eyes: sparkling, bright and loving.

In my dream, I was in some kind of room with other people – the room had tables but I don't remember eating. When I saw Eric, I went up to hug him. At first, he wasn't real, and my arms went through him as if he were a ghost. I was disappointed not to be able to hug him when all of a sudden he had a human body and I was able to hug him. He never said anything, but had a bit of a concerned look on his face. He then turned to leave and as he was approaching the door, I said to him, "Give Jesus a hug for me."

He went out of the building and I saw him following my parents who were walking by the window with close relatives. They never knew that Eric was following them. And that's where the dream ended.

The dream was amazingly real! Eric had been so real! I had hugged him hard. He never said anything, but just his presence had been a comfort. It made me wonder if God had sent him to ease some kind of pain that was just around the corner – letting me know that God was aware of it and would be present with me. At first I thought it might be the pain of losing one of my parents. But the weeks and months passed and nothing happened to them. Then five months later, I realized that the pain Eric came to prepare me for was my own, as I was suddenly diagnosed with stage 4 melanoma.

Eric came as a type of messenger to let me know that God was in control and that I didn't need to worry. God would be with me, and He would also comfort my parents in yet another trial with one of their kids.

Lumps and Pinky Fingers

February 2, 2011

<u>STONE:</u>

God miraculously orchestrated the removal of a lump on my chest wall through a tennis accident with my pinky finger.

For two years I had a lump on my right chest wall (between my breast and my armpit). Four doctors saw it and thought it was just a benign, fatty cyst that was fine to leave alone. But at one point it started to grow in size to the point where it started to hurt when wearing a bra or buckling my seatbelt. As it grew, I had an inner urging from the Lord to go see my primary doctor, Sennie Anderson. The next day I got a notice in the mail that I was overdue for an appointment with her. I had never gotten such a notice in the seven years we had lived in Grants Pass! So I felt fairly certain that this was from the Lord and that I should pursue seeing her.

Steve was not as sure, thinking I should rather see my Dermatologist in Medford, Dr. Naverson, who had said he'd take out the cyst if it ever bothered me. So I called his office but the receptionist said he was completely booked until June/July, which was still 5-6 months away. With the urgency I was feeling, I told the Lord, "If You want me to get this taken out earlier, You are going to have to orchestrate me seeing Sennie."

Well, that next Saturday I was playing tennis and while at net I put up my hand to protect myself as my opponent made a really hard overhead smash. The ball hit my left pinky finger, tearing the extensor tendon. Since it was a weekend I had to go to the Immediate Care Center rather than to my regular doctor.

While I was in the waiting room, I saw posted the names of the two doctors who were on call that day. I thought to myself, "Too bad Sennie doesn't work here." I was called into a patient room where I waited for a doctor to come in. And who knocks on the door and walks in but Sennie Anderson! I was so blown away that I said, "What are you doing here?! You don't work here! Your name wasn't even on the board!"

"I came in just for you," she joked. How little did she know how true that statement was! She told me she was working some weekends at the Immediate Care Center to supplement her hours and experience. Wow! The lengths that God would go to in order to have me see her.

After she treated my finger, I asked her if I could inquire about one more unrelated medical problem. She very willingly said yes. So I showed her the growth on my chest wall. She said she thought it should come out, and she said that on Monday, when she would be back in her office at Mountain View Family Practice, she would write a referral for me to see a surgeon in town.

I went in on Monday, got a referral to Dr. Cory Fawcett, and went to see him on Thursday for a consult. When Cory saw the lump, he said it should be taken out immediately. He then said, "How about right now?" Evidently the first consult is a bit longer than other appointments, and since it was right before lunch he was willing to take the extra time if needed.

So within two weeks of me praying, "Lord, if You want this taken out, You are going to have to make this happen," He did! Dr. Fawcett thought the mass was suspicious and wanted to send it off for a biopsy. I had peace, however, that no matter what the results might be, that I could trust God, because of how He had orchestrated all the details in order to get the mass removed. He was with me and I could rely on Him.

A Special Sleepover

<u>STONE:</u>

God gave Psalm 34 to Nika and me at the same time for encouragement in my cancer.

The weekend after I learned I had advanced melanoma, Nika came down from Corban University to spend the weekend with me. Steve was overseas at the time and she wanted to spend some time with me to process it all and to be an encouragement to me.

Her first night home, she asked if I wanted to do a sleepover. "Sure," I said. So she brought her Bible in and curled up on the bed next to me. We read separately for a few minutes, our backs to one another. Then she said, "Mom, you've got to read Psalm 34:19. It says,

> *"The righteous person may have many troubles,*
> *but the Lord delivers him from them all."*

I looked over at her and said, "Did you know where I was reading?" She said no. She then leaned over my shoulder and saw that I, too, was reading Psalm 34. Unbelievable! God wanted us to know with certainty that this Psalm was from Him for our situation. In it was a reminder of how we were to act, and how He would act toward us:

- praising God at all times
- looking to Him and being radiant
- His deliverance
- His protection for those who fear Him
- His closeness to the brokenhearted
- His redemption for His servants

God sometimes gives life verses. This Psalm would be God's reminder to us for my season with cancer: "I'll get you through this."

The Tumult of the City

March 2, 2011

STONE:

"Keep that smile in the tumult of the city" – an angel's encouragement at the Los Altos Library.

Steve and I were down in the Bay Area for my first appointment with Dr. Algazi at the UCSF Melanoma Center. There was quite a bit of discouraging news, the worst being the very real possibility of having stage 4 melanoma rather than just stage 3, which would only give me a matter of months to live. Fighting the traffic in San Francisco and being surrounded by concrete and steel made me feel like I was almost on a different planet.

I told Steve I needed some quiet time alone with the Lord, which was hard to get at his folks' house, so we drove over to the Los Altos Library. I found my own little cubical to hide away in and then poured out my heart to God in my journal saying, "Lord, speak to my heart right now. I am so tired and spent, and not being home in Oregon has been difficult as well. Lord, what do You want to say to me?"

He brought to mind the verses in Hebrews 12:1-3 which encouraged me to throw off unbelief and doubt, keeping my eyes fixed on the One who overcame. While I was considering these verses, Nika called, so I hurriedly made my way out of the library and talked to her for a bit. On the way back in, a man sitting by the entrance caught my attention as I approached. He had no books in his hands, and he was looking directly at me as if he was wanting to tell me something. When I got close he said to me, "Keep that smile in the tumult of the city."

I opened the door to the library slowly, thinking about the man's words. "Tumult of the city?" Who today ever says the word "tumult"? How did he know I was struggling with going in and out of the city? When I had been talking to Nika on the phone I had been far enough away that there was no way he could have possibly heard what I was saying. And I didn't remember saying anything to her about the city. But this man, not knowing my situation, responded to the question I had asked the Lord just a few minutes earlier, "What do You want to say to me?"

I went back to the front door a minute later to look for the man, but he was gone. I believe that God sent His messenger to talk directly to my heart and to encourage me in my hour of need. God wanted me to keep smiling in the tumult of the city. This word from the Lord encouraged me that whole year, every time I had to make a trip to the Bay Area to see my doctors. God was trustworthy and He was with me. Now that brings a smile.

Will I Live?

October 22-23, 2011

STONE:

I asked God in Oregon about whether I was going to live another year. A man told Steve that same morning at Hamilton Congregational Church in Massachusetts, "She will live."

In October 2011, I flew back from the East Coast for a PET CT and an appointment with Dr. Algazi. Steve stayed on for one more week in Massachusetts to speak at the last of our supporting churches. Unfortunately the cancer was growing again and the tumor above my right kidney was very large. My father-in-law drove me back up to Oregon and then returned home, and Nika came down from Corban University to spend time with me over the weekend.

Saturday night I had a dream that was vivid and very real. In it I saw people's faces flashing before me who were going to die in the upcoming year, 2012. I didn't see my face, but faces were still flashing by me when I woke up.

At around 7:30 a.m. I went down to our basement for my quiet time and pondered the dream. Then I asked, "Lord, am I going to live?" I listened but didn't hear a yes or no from the Lord. I wondered if the reason I couldn't hear God's voice on this was because I was so wanting to hear a "yes" that it could be blocking out His still small voice that might want to tell me something different.

On the way to church, I told Nika about my dream and then I asked her, "Do you have a sense from the Lord whether I am going to live or die this year?" She said she hadn't heard from Him one way or the other.

Later that day, Steve called from Massachusetts to catch me up on his day and his time that morning sharing about our work at the First Congregational Church in Hamilton. Almost as an afterthought he said that after he finished speaking at the combined Sunday School class, a man came up to him and said, "I have something I want you to tell Laura." He was emotional and had tears in his eyes and it took him a few seconds before he was able to compose himself and speak again. Then he said, "Tell Laura – she will live." He then turned and walked away and Steve didn't see him again.

As Steve passed on to me the man's message, I couldn't believe my ears. I had just asked the Lord that morning, "Am I going to live?", and here God had answered my question through a man we didn't even know 3,000 miles away. I asked Steve what time the man had come up and talked to him. He said it was at 10:30 a.m., right after he finished speaking. This was exactly the time on the West Coast I was pouring out my heart to the Lord and waiting to hear His reply.

Well, God did answer, and in a way that only He could do. I was going to LIVE! ☺

Putting His Plan into Play

November 1 and November 5, 2011

STONE:

God started killing off my tumor the day He told me, "She will live," and orchestrated a surgery for it's removal.

When God told me through the man on the East Coast that I would live, I really didn't know what to expect. I was now confident that God would get me through 2012, but I wasn't sure if I'd live much past that or whether He intended to heal me completely. But the same day that Steve called me with those sweet words, "She will live," God started putting into play His plan of how He was going to accomplish this.

That afternoon I started having pain below my right ribcage, in the area where my largest tumor was located. Up until that point I had never had ANY pain associated with my cancer. The pain started as a cramp which made it difficult to inhale. All that next week the pain steadily increased to the point that the following Saturday night, Steve came into our bathroom at one in the morning to find me on my hands and knees, writhing in pain. He quickly got me into the car and we started for the emergency room in Grants Pass. But on the way we decided we needed to go to San Francisco instead, since the doctors at UCSF knew my whole medical situation. So we drove through a snowstorm that night up over Siskiyou Pass in order to go to the Emergency Room in San Francisco.

Tests revealed that I had necrosis in the large tumor by my kidney, which meant that the tumor was growing so quickly on the outside that the blood supply to the inside was insufficient and that part was dying. Dr. Algazi had never given surgery as an option, saying that at stage 4 the cancer would just grow somewhere else. But this situation was different. They said if the tumor wasn't removed, I was in danger of hemorrhaging internally and bleeding out.

Although the doctor had recommended an immediate removal, the soonest they could schedule me for the surgery was a month away. I pleaded with the receptionist to try to get it sooner. She said it was a long shot, but that she would see if it might be possible for the upcoming Monday, only three days away.

God worked out all the details, and at 7:30 a.m. on November 2nd, the largest tumor was removed from my side, as well as my right kidney and adrenal gland. This was just 15 days after God had said through the man on the East Coast, "She will live."

I just love the verse in Isaiah 55:8 that says,

> *"For my thoughts are not your thoughts,*
> *neither are your ways my ways,'*
> *declares the Lord."*

God had started putting His plan into play and nothing could stop Him.

Horses and Chariots

January 20 and February 21, 2012

STONE:

God leads me to try Bill Henderson's Cancer Protocol and encourages me that He would have victory over my cancer.

In January 2012, I got another email from Stephen Peterson, who attended one of our supporting churches in Connecticut. Once again he implored me to start following the recommendations in the book, "Cancer-Free: Your Guide to Gentle, Non-Toxic Healing," by Bill Henderson. He had even purchased the book for me, telling me in October when we were at his church, "Don't you realize you're going to die if you just keep taking the drugs your doctors are giving you?"

Steve and I both read the book and the alternative cancer treatments made sense – cut off how the cancer grows and you won't have cancer. We bought the supplements before our trip to San Francisco in November for an appointment with Dr. Algazi, but when we showed him the alternative treatments, he recommended not doing it. He said it might interfere with the drug I was currently on, Zelboraf.

But in early January, we discovered my cancer was growing again, and another lump was removed from my chest wall. Zelboraf was not only proving ineffective in holding back the cancer, it also had a lot of harsh side effects, even at a quarter of the recommended dosage, which was all I could tolerate. And there weren't any other drugs to try or trials that I qualified for. That's when Peterson's email came, once again urging me to try Henderson's protocol. Peterson even recommended me calling a man who had followed the protocol and was now cancer free from melanoma. After talking to the man on the phone, I felt in my heart that God was saying, "This is the time." I had another 6 ½ weeks until my next PET CT scan, and this protocol was supposed to work in that time frame.

The protocol demanded a radical change in diet: no sugar, no dairy, no meat, no gluten, and no processed foods. There were also a number of different supplements I needed to take. A month into the protocol, I was having a morning quiet time and came to the passage in Joshua 11:6 where God talks to Joshua about how He was going to defeat the Northern Kingdoms. God told him,

> *"Do not be afraid of them, because by this time*
> *tomorrow I will hand all of them, slain, over to Israel.*
> *You are to hamstring their horses and burn their*
> *chariots."*

God's role was that He would be responsible for defeating Joshua's enemy. Joshua's job was not to fear, but to take out the way the enemy was planning to win - removing their horses and chariots. God impressed on me that the same was true in my fight against melanoma. He was the one who would give the victory. What He wanted me to do was not to fear, but to disable the strength of how the cancer could beat me (through sugars, an acidic environment, etc.). He encouraged me that I would be doing my part by following Henderson's protocol.

So that morning, God impressed on me that He would have victory over my cancer. I just needed to be faithful and hamstring my cancer's horses.

This Just Doesn't Happen

March 8, 2012

<u>STONE:</u>

Cancer Free!

Four and a half months after God told me through the man on the East Coast that I would live, my oncologist, Dr. Algazi walked into the examining room where I sat and said, "This is very unusual. There is no sign of cancer on your PET CT." He then added, "This just doesn't happen."

With a bit of trepidation, we explained that since we had seen that the Zelboraf was no longer working, we decided to follow the recommendations in the book we had shown him previously, "Cancer-Free" by Bill Henderson. He wasn't real happy about that, but he couldn't refute the results, and said, "Whatever you're doing, just keep doing it!" We told him we were praising God for this clear scan, because we knew that He was the one who had answered our prayers.

After I left Dr. Algazi's office, I stepped into the elevator and let out a huge shout of joy that I'm sure resounded throughout the whole building! God is indeed faithful and He keeps His promises! I was cancer free! I would live!

Buy the Tickets!

March 30, 2012

<u>STONE:</u>

God confirms my going to Nepal with Steve in October with direct answers to my food and health concerns.

Right after I was declared cancer free in March 2012, Steve started talking about me going with him to Nepal in October. He wanted me to see the country, help out at a Luke Partnership translation workshop, and trek with him to Annapurna Base Camp for our 25th wedding anniversary. Now that we were empty nesters and I was cancer free, he assumed we would be able to start traveling together overseas. I on the other hand was concerned about the trip from the start, that my cancer might return due to not being able to control my special cancer-fighting diet, both during our time in Kathmandu as well as on the trek.

The end of the month came and it was decision time. The tickets were reserved and we had to pay for them by the following day. I prayed that night that God would give me a dream about whether to go or not. Nothing. The next morning Steve mentioned he was going to go ahead and purchase the tickets. I voiced how concerned I was about having to worry if there would be fresh vegetables, cottage cheese, flaxseed oil, etc. I also told him I thought it could create a rift between us if getting things for my diet proved to be a problem. Steve replied, "Why would God heal you if it wasn't for the purpose of being able to go back overseas again and be part of the ministry?" He also mentioned how this trip would provide a good opportunity to check out Nepal as a possible ongoing ministry location. I felt a bit better after talking, but told Steve I still needed until noon to decide. I needed to hear directly from the Lord on this.

After getting back from my physical therapy session in town (8-9 a.m.), I went down to my "cave" (our workout room), and asked the Lord to make it clear whether I should go to Nepal or not. On the way down, I grabbed John Eckhardt's book, "Daily Declarations for Spiritual Warfare". Vicki Bauer had given it to me two weeks earlier for my 50th birthday and this was the first time I felt led to read it. I turned to that day's reading (March 30) and the title said, "I will guide you continually." A good start! And then it went on to speak directly to my concerns and fears by saying:

> "I will be your hiding place and I will protect you from trouble. I will instruct you and teach you in the way you should go. I will counsel you with my loving eye on you. *I will always guide you and provide good things to eat when you are in the desert. I will make you healthy...*"

The moment I read this, the Lord put my fearful heart to rest. He was telling me that He would provide the good things that I needed to keep me healthy during my stay in Nepal. I could trust Him. Once again, God's voice and His leading were clear and unmistakable.

I went upstairs and with confidence told Steve, "Buy the tickets!"

Stubborn as Jonah

November 17, 2012

STONE:

God calling me back to Nepal (as with stubborn Jonah) in January 2013.

A few weeks after my first trip to Nepal in the fall of 2012, the talk of going back again early the following year came up. If I were to go with Steve, that would allow him to stay for a few months and he would be able to run two workshops instead of just one. It would also give us both some time to learn Nepali, which would especially help Steve in his work with the nationals.

Somewhere deep in my heart I knew this was the right thing to do. But I was feeling a bit like Jonah who wanted to run in a different direction and follow his own will instead of the Lord's. So one morning in my quiet time I asked God to make His will clearly known to me concerning whether I should go to Nepal in January 2013. In my daily reading I was at Isaiah 55 and came to verses 11 and 12 which say:

> *"So is my word that goes out from my mouth:*
> *It will not return to me empty,*
> *but will accomplish what I desire*
> *and achieve the purpose for which I sent it.*
> *You will go out in joy*
> *and be led forth in peace;*
> *the mountains and hills*
> *will burst into song before you,*
> *and all the trees of the field*
> *will clap their hands."*

I got the message. But I didn't want to pay attention to what God was saying to my heart, that I was to "go out in joy."

I left my quiet time and drove downtown to bring the blue car into Tom's Auto for some repairs. While I waited at Dutch Brothers for the work to be done, I did my women's Bible study lesson which was in Priscilla Shirer's study going through the book of Jonah. In that day's lesson I was totally convicted that I was being a "Jonah". Everything (the wind, a huge fish, a shade tree) and everyone (sailors and Ninivites) in the book of Jonah was doing God's will EXCEPT Jonah himself! Jonah preferred his own comfort over the conversion of many souls.

Right as I was feeling the most convicted at Dutch Brothers, Steve called and said he just received a phone call from Jeff Webster who thought it would be a good thing for us to go to Nepal in January and stay a few months. He said that knowing a bit of Nepali would help Steve in his work, and the extra time would allow him to consultant check Psalms with the Branchu team.

God was gently but obviously confirming that His will was for me to go. As soon as I surrendered my will to His, He gave me a joy and excitement that was not my own. After picking up the car, I even headed over to Ross to try to find some clothes so that we could stay warm in Kathmandu's cold winter season.

God was right. I would "go out in joy and be led forth in peace".

Not on My Radar

January 24 and 29, 2013

STONE:

God leads me to teach Elementary P.E. at the Kathmandu International Study Center in Nepal.

Obeying the Lord's call to go back to Nepal for the second time, I arrived in Kathmandu in January 2013. I wasn't sure what God wanted me to do during my two months there, but I was open to His leading. I started language learning and tried my hand at helping Steve consultant check Scripture with the Sukkha and Acacia teams. Although it was encouraging to help the teams, I still felt like God might have something else He wanted me to do during my time there, so I continued to pray for wisdom.

Three days later we went to the international church service held weekly at the Kathmandu International Study Center (KISC). During announcements, Leslie, the school principal stood up and said they were in desperate need of a certified teacher who was a native English speaker and who could commit to teach the 3rd grade class for one to two months. In two days the current teacher was flying unexpectedly back to the States to be with her dying father, and they needed a replacement until she would be able to return.

For the whole rest of the church service, the Holy Spirit kept impressing on my heart that I was supposed to offer my services. I never really wanted to teach at KISC or even to help out there. That was totally not on my radar of what I thought I would be doing. I had been considering the possibility of helping feed the poor or helping out at an orphanage, but I hadn't wanted to get involved at the school for missionary kids. But God had other plans and I followed His leading.

I went up to Leslie after the service and told her I'd be willing to fill in for the teacher during her absence. I told her my teaching degree was for middle school and secondary P.E., but that I'd be willing to teach the 3rd grade class. She told me to come to the school office the next morning and we could talk more then.

When I arrived, Leslie told me she wanted me to teach elementary P.E. instead of the 3rd grade class. She said another parent had also volunteered to teach that class, and she really wanted to give the current P.E. teacher the opportunity to observe other schools in Kathmandu to broaden her base of teaching ideas. It was something the P.E. teacher had requested for some time and Leslie had never been able to give her the time off to do it.

At first I was thrown for a loop. Wasn't I responding to a desperate call to teach 3rd grade? But as I pondered it, I realized that God was using the call for help to get me to serve at the school in the area that I loved the most: physical education. God took my willingness and pointed me in a direction that used both my gifts and my passion. It ended up being a great experience and a blessing for everyone.

The Ideal Flat

February 19 and 24, 2013

<u>STONE:</u>

God provides a perfect apartment for us in Kathmandu.

After living in the Oatley's guest flat in Kathmandu for a month during the winter, Steve and I knew we would never want to do that again. It was on the ground floor which was at least ten degrees colder than the upper floors. No sun came in our windows, and we only had limited propane for the heater to try to thaw ourselves in the evenings. Besides the cold, we always felt vulnerable to theft as we weren't allowed to lock our flat when we were out. We considered other places we could possibly rent on future trips, but realized there really were no good options.

Then came the idea of getting our own small flat where we could stay while in Kathmandu and maybe rent out when gone. It would have to be around $150/month as we'd only be in Nepal about four months a year. I wrote in my journal three things that I wanted:

1. a quiet place with greenery and privacy
2. an apartment off the ground level
3. an apartment that gets sun in the windows

The next day Steve and I found a local real estate agent and told him what we were hoping to find for a certain price. Steve went around with him and saw three run-down places that were ground level, not secure, and all over $200/month. After this, we were pretty discouraged and were thinking it might not be possible to have our own place. However later that afternoon, Barb Naylor emailed us about an older couple, David and Ann McConkey, who would be leaving their apartment at the end of August after 30 years in Nepal. She said we could go over and check it out that evening.

The flat was ideal. It was situated at the end of a relatively quiet lane. It was on the third floor with sun coming in the master bedroom and a porch off that side as well. There was also a small guest bedroom, living room, kitchen and bathroom – just the size we were hoping for. We'd have access to the roof, which looked out at the mountains, and there were some trees and garden areas around the house. We also found out that the landlord who lived below had been an army officer so the flat would be protected and safe from theft.

The big "hitch" was that the landlords were planning on raising the rent before the next tenants moved in. They had been keeping it low at 15,000 rupees/month for the McConkey's for a number of years without raising it. They told us the flat next to theirs just went for 23,000 rupees and wasn't as nice as theirs. They said they'd give us their decision in a few days. I prayed that God would have them only go up just a little (to a maximum of 17,000 rupees, which was just under $200). A few days later we got their decision and were thrilled when they told us their monthly price: 17,000 rupees!

We were able to furnish the flat by purchasing most of the McConkey's belongings, and they gave us a great deal on everything. We picked up the last few items we needed four days later when a man had to leave the country unexpectedly, and we were given first dibs on his furniture. God provided us a new home away from home!

An Early Morning Conversation

March 21, 2103

STONE:

A God-ordained conversation with the Lord at 2:00 a.m.

One day I drove my neighbor Shelley to Medford so that she could do some shopping there. On the way home, she mentioned how she kept waking up at 2:00 a.m., then 3:30 a.m., then 4:00 a.m. each night. Finally she'd get back to sleep. While she was talking I kept thinking to myself, "Maybe God is wanting to talk to her." What was convicting for me was that a few nights before, I was restless and had woken up frequently, but hadn't thought of listening to the Lord. What if He had been wanting to get my attention?

Anyway, the following night I woke up at some point and went to the bathroom. While there I thought to myself, "If it is exactly 2:00 a.m. on Steve's digital clock when I go back to bed, I'll know that God woke me up to talk to me."

When I went back to our bedroom I looked at the clock and couldn't believe my eyes: 2:00 a.m.!!! So I lay down and talked with God for a few minutes, but then realized that I'd quickly fall back asleep if I didn't change my position! So I sat up, turned on my flashlight, grabbed a pen and piece of paper, and listened. Here is what transpired:

(Laura) "Speak, Lord, Your servant is listening."

(Spirit) "I want you. I don't want you to love and follow Me for others' sake, but for My sake, to know and bless Me. You are still too concerned about what others think – doing things to please them. But it's all about Me. Life is about Me, living is about Me, your daily breath is about Me."

(Laura) "Lord, would You teach me what it means to be led by You, to be filled by You?"

(Spirit) "Why? To bless you or to bless Me? For your glory or My glory? Pride comes before a fall. Be all about Me and nothing more. Be all about knowing Me, and nothing more. That is where abiding begins and where life truly is."

(Laura) "Lord, I've been wanting to know what You have for me, what You want me to do."

(Spirit) "Start with just knowing Me and waiting on Me to fill and lead you. You can't serve Me when you are about you. You need to be overflowing with Me."

(Laura) "Lord, forgive me for making it all about me, for loving things in this life more than loving You – especially after all You've shown me the last two years, after all You've done for me."

(Spirit) "I saved your life for a purpose."

(Laura) "What purpose, Lord?"

(Spirit) "You'll know in time. Right now just enjoy Me, seek Me. Hunger and thirst after the Great Pearl, the only lasting thing. Your Egypt is nothing, absolutely nothing, in comparison."

(Laura) "Thank You, Lord, that You love me enough to wake me up, to not let me go my own way. You continue to amaze me by Your love."

(Spirit) "Oh, there is so little that you know of My love yet. You just wait!"

(Laura) "Praise You, Lord. Thank You."

Final Words

Fifty years and ticking. Until my final day comes, I will keep recording God moments in my journal and adding to the plate of memorial stones in my living room. Whenever I might leave this earth, what I want is for people to remember these stories and say, "Wow, our God is awesome!"

What really motivated me to share my God stories with you was the hope that you would get the idea that you could do this yourself – recording your own God moments so that your kids and grandkids will know how great our God is. You don't need years of journals to pour through – just think back and remember the times God has intervened on your behalf. And if you can't find flat, round stones to record your God moments, you can use slips of nice paper and put them on a plate or in a jar. The important thing is that we pass on the things God has done for us so that the next generation will know Him and trust Him. As it says in Psalm 102:18:

> *"Let this be written for a future generation,*
> *that a people not yet created*
> *may praise the Lord."*

About the Author

Laura Payne is an ordinary woman following an extra-ordinary God. She is married to Steve and has two great kids, Nika and Kevin. She and Steve have been working with Wycliffe Bible Translators and The Seed Company for the last 25 years. They currently make their home in Grants Pass, Oregon, but travel frequently overseas.

Notes for Your "Twelve Stone" Project

Jot down below some of the God moments from your life as you consider starting your own "Twelve Stone" project, so that future generations will know of God's love and faithfulness to you!

_____